KT-477-292

love your
library

Buckinghamshire Libraries

Search, renew or reserve online 24/7
www.buckscc.gov.uk/libraries

24 hour renewal line
0303 123 0035

Enquiries
01296 382415

follow us **twitter**

@Bucks_Libraries

written and researched by

MATTHEW HANCOCK

15 361 689 9

Contents

INTRODUCTION 4

Lisbon at a glance 7   Itineraries 8

BEST OF LISBON 12

The big sights 14   Cafés 22
Museums and galleries 16   Shopping 24
Eating out................................. 18   Parks and gardens 26
Nightlife................................... 20   Squares....................................... 28

PLACES 30

1 The Baixa and Rossio 32   7 Belém and Ajuda 90
2 The Sé, Castelo and Alfama ...44   8 Avenida, Parque Eduardo VII
3 Chiado and Cais do Sodré 58   and the Gulbenkian.............. 98
4 Bairro Alto and São Bento 66   9 Parque das Nações 110
5 Estrela, Lapa and Santos...... 78   10 Sintra 116
6 Alcântara and the docks 84   11 The Lisbon coast 126

ACCOMMODATION 132

ESSENTIALS 142

Arrival.....................................144   Chronology 151
Getting around 144   Portuguese 152
Directory A–Z..........................147   Index..156
Festivals and events...............150

INTRODUCTION TO
LISBON

Set across a series of hills overlooking the broad estuary of the Rio Tejo (River Tagus), Lisbon's stunning location and effortless beauty immediately strike most first-time visitors. It's an instantly likeable place, a big city, with a population of around two million, but one that remains human enough in pace and scale to be easily taken in over a long weekend. That said, many visitors visit again and again, smitten by a combination of old-world charm and cosmopolitan vibrancy that makes it one of Europe's most exciting cities.

RUA AUGUSTA, BAIXA

PORTAS DO SOL, ALFAMA

Best places for alfresco dining

The best way to soak up Lisbon's atmosphere is to grab an outdoor table and sit back with a coffee or something more substantial. Sample tapas at *Pharmacia*, in a fine little garden overlooking the Tagus (p.74), or enjoy a pizza-with-a-view at riverside *Casanova* (see p.55). It is harder to find a lovelier lunch spot than the sleek, riverside *Á Margem* (see p.97). Alternatively, head to one of Lisbon's squares or *miradouros* (viewpoints), many of which have cafés, bars or restaurants, such as *Portas do Sol* (above, see p.57).

Although one of the EU's least expensive capitals, Lisbon was once one of the continent's wealthiest, controlling a maritime empire that stretched from Brazil to Macau. The iconic Torre de Belém, Mosteiro dos Jerónimos and dramatic Moorish castle survive from these times, though many other buildings were destroyed in the Great Earthquake of 1755. Today, much of the historic centre – the Baixa, Chiado and Bairro Alto – dates from the late eighteenth and nineteenth centuries. The biggest attraction in these quarters is the street life: nothing beats watching the city's comings and goings from a pavement café over a powerful *bica* coffee or Portuguese beer.

If you're fit enough to negotiate its hills, Lisbon is a great place to explore on foot: get off the beaten track and you'll find atmospheric neighbourhoods sheltering aromatic *pastelarias* (patisseries), traditional shops, and shuttered houses faced with beautiful *azulejo* tiles. Getting around by public transport can be fun in itself, whether you're cranking uphill on one of the city's ancient trams, riding a ferry across the Rio Tejo, or speeding across town on the metro, whose stations are decorated with adventurous contemporary art.

Lisbon also boasts excellent museums – from the Gulbenkian, with its amazing collection of arts through the ages, to the Berardo, whose modern paintings are the envy of Europe, via the Museu Nacional de Arte Antiga, the national gallery, with top

When to visit

Lisbon is comfortably warm from April to October (average daily temperature 20–28ºC), with cooling Atlantic breezes making it less hot than Mediterranean cities on the same latitude. Most Lisbon residents take their holidays in July and August (27–28ºC), which means that some shops, bars and restaurants close for the period and the local beaches are heaving. Lower temperatures of 22–26ºC mean September and October are good times to visit, as is June, when the city enjoys its main festivals. Even in midwinter it is rarely cold and, as one of Europe's sunniest capitals, the sun usually appears at some stage to light up the city.

Portuguese and European masterpieces.

Lisbon's eclectic nightlife scene ranges from the traditional fado clubs of the Alfama district to glitzy venues in the Bairro Alto and along the riverfront, many of them playing African and Brazilian beats influenced by immigrants from Portugal's former colonies.

Elsewhere, the city offers a fascinating mishmash of the traditional and cutting edge: chequered-tiled bars full of old-timers supping brandies adjacent to boutiquey clubs pumping out the latest sounds; tiny *tascas* with bargain menus scrawled on boards rubbing shoulders with designer

restaurants eyeing the latest Michelin awards, and tiny stores that wrap handmade products in paper and string overlooking gleaming shopping malls.

Should city life begin to pall, take the train out to the beautiful hilltop town of Sintra, whose lush wooded heights and royal palaces comprise a UNESCO World Heritage Site. Alternatively, the lively resorts of Estoril and Cascais are just half an hour away, with the best beaches lying south of the city, along the Costa da Caparica, where Atlantic breakers crash on kilometre after kilometre of superb dune-backed sands.

SANTA ENGRÁCIA

LISBON AT A GLANCE

>> EATING

You are never far from a restaurant in Lisbon. For diversity, head to the **Bairro Alto** district where you'll find an eclectic array of inexpensive diners alongside ultrahip venues. The **Baixa** caters to Lisbon's workers and has a whole street, Rua das Portas de Santo Antão, largely given over to seafood restaurants. International flavours can be sampled by the Tejo at the **Parque das Nações** and the dockside developments at **Santa Apolonia** and **Doca de Santo Amaro**, while fashionistas head to the cool haunts of **Cais do Sodré**. Some of the best dining experiences, however, are in local neighbourhood restaurants highlighted in the Guide.

>> DRINKING

The most historic cafés are scattered throughout the **Baixa** and **Chiado** districts where you'll find locals getting their caffeine fixes throughout the day. You can also get beer, wine or food at these places, though many bars only open after dark (see below). Portuguese beers – largely Sagres and Superbock – are inexpensive and recommended, while local wines are invariably excellent. Worth sampling too are local brandies; the white variety of port, which makes an excellent aperitif; and a powerful cherry brandy called *ginginha* – several bars in the Baixa specialize in the stuff. Finally,

don't miss trying a *caipirinha*, a Brazilian cocktail made from distilled sugar cane, sugar and lime juice.

>> SHOPPING

Suburban Lisbon has some of Europe's largest shopping malls, but the city centre is a pleasing mixture of quirky local stores and smaller independent outlets. The top end of **Avenida da Liberdade** features the likes of Armani and Louis Vuitton, while Chiado is the place to head for glass and jewellery. Antique shops cluster round **São Bento**, **Príncipe Real** and **Campo de Santa Clara**, while off-the-wall clothing and accessories are to be found in the independent boutiques of the **Bairro Alto**. **Santos** has become the district of design, with several stores dedicated to contemporary jewellery and cutting-edge home products.

>> NIGHTLIFE

Lisbon has a pulsating nightlife, with the highest concentration of clubs and bars in the **Bairro Alto**. Many locals prefer the less frenetic vibe of the **Cais do Sodré** district, which has a handful of cool clubs and happening bars; while the city's biggest clubs are to be found near the river, especially *Lux* near **Santa Apolonia** and the upmarket venues of **Alcântara**. There are various excellent live music venues, with the **Bairro Alto** and **Alfama** famed for their fado houses.

OUR RECOMMENDATIONS FOR WHERE TO EAT, DRINK AND SHOP ARE LISTED AT THE END OF EACH PLACES CHAPTER.

Day One in Lisbon

Café Suíça > p.43. Join the bustle of the central square's best café, the best place to people-watch.

1 The Baixa > p.35. Head down main Rua da Augusta and explore the lively streets and cafés of the Baixa grid.

2 Chiado > p.58. Stroll up Rua do Carmo and Rua Garrett where many of Lisbon's best shops can be found.

Lunch > p.64. At *Leitaria Académica*, with a simple menu and tables outside a lovely square.

3 Tram #28 > p.53. This is Lisbon's most famous tram route, grinding back through the Baixa and up towards the Castelo through the Alfama.

4 Castelo de São Jorge > p.48. Walk up to the ruined Moorish castle, the heart of historic Lisbon.

5 Alfama > p.51. Take the steps into the Alfama, Lisbon's village within a city where traditional life still holds sway.

6 Museu do Fado > p.52. Gain an insight into the history and sounds of Portugal's distinctive music at this informative museum.

Dinner > p.57. Try one of the Alfama's fado houses, where you can dine while listening to live music; *A Baiuca* is a good place to start.

Drinks > p.57. End the night by the riverside at *Lux*, one of Europe's coolest clubs.

Day Two in Lisbon

1 Museu Calouste Gulbenkian > p.103. Take the metro to this superb museum displaying arts and crafts from the time of the Ancient Egyptians to the French Impressionists.

2 Parque Eduardo VII > p.104. It is a short walk from the museums to Lisbon's main central park famed for its Estufas – hothouses filled with exotic plants.

3 Praça do Comércio > p.32. Take the metro or bus to the city's graceful riverside square and take the riverside path west for ten minutes to Cais do Sodré.

Lunch > p.60. Have lunch at one of the many food stalls in the Mercado da Ribeira, Lisbon's main market.

4 Mosteiro dos Jerónimos > p.91. Take the tram to Belém's fantastic monastery, built to give thanks to the success of Portugal's great navigators.

5 Berardo Collection > p.93. Don't miss this superb collection of modern art, featuring the likes of Andy Warhol and Paula Rego.

6 Torre de Belém > p.94. Climb the elaborate sixteenth-century riverside tower that has become the symbol of the city.

Dinner > p.73. *Cervejaria da Trindade*, a cavernous beer hall serving great seafood.

Drinks > p.75. Stick around the Bairro Alto and wait for the nightlife to crank up at its hundreds of little bars and clubs.

Lisbon **viewpoints**

Built on seven hills, Lisbon has some fantastic *miradouros*, or viewpoints, each with its own distinctive outlook over the city's skyline – here we list the best, along with some other dramatic vantage points.

1 Miradouro de Santa Luzia > p.48. The best place to see over the terracotta rooftops of the Alfama and the eastern riverfront.

2 São Vicente de Fora > p.50. Climb to the top of this historic church for dizzy views over the eastern city from its extensive roof.

3 Castelo > p.48. Not quite Lisbon's highest hill, but climb around the ramparts to see all sides of the city.

4 Parque Eduardo VII > p.104. The top of the park offers an exhilarating panorama encompassing Lisbon and beyond.

Lunch > p.109. Chill out by a lake at *A Linha d'Água*, which serves good-value buffet lunches at the top of the park.

5 Miradouro da Graça > p.50. Superb views over the Castelo and the city beyond can be had from this breezy terrace by the church of Graça.

6 Miradouro de São Pedro de Alcântara > p.66. A broad, tree-lined viewpoint from where you can gaze down on the Baixa and the castle opposite.

7 Miradouro de Santa Catarina > p.70. Tucked-away *miradouro* with sweeping views over the Tejo, a popular hangout for Lisbon's alternative crowd.

Dinner > p.75. *Noobai* is hidden under the lip of Miradouro de Santa Catarina and serves inexpensive food and drinks.

Lisbon **for families**

Lisbon is very family friendly and children are welcomed everywhere. Below are some of the best attractions for those with kids of any age.

1 Street lifts > p.60. There are several wacky street lifts up Lisbon's steepest hills; Elevador da Bica is the most fun.

2 Oceanário > p.112. One of the largest in Europe, this stunning building has sharks, rays, otters, penguins and fish galore.

3 Pavilhão do Conhecimento > p.112. This science museum has fantastic hands-on experiments and challenges for people of all ages, together with informative exhibits.

Lunch > p.115. The traffic-free restaurants of Parque das Nações are great for kids – one of the best places for an inexpensive lunch is *Azul Profundo*.

4 Boat trips > p.146. Take a leisurely cruise up the Tejo to see the city from the river.

5 Museu da Marioneta > p.81. From medieval marionettes to contemporary satirical puppets, this museum trumpets an art form that satisfied children long before computer games.

6 Museu da Carris > p.87. Lisbon's trams are great fun to ride on, but here kids can clamber about trams, buses and metro trains with fewer crowds.

7 Caparica > p.129. Lisbon's best beaches are just south of the city, great at any time of the year for a walk or day by the sea.

8 Sintra > p.116. Horse and carriage rides, castles and fantasy palaces make this a great day out for any family.

Dinner > p.41. With lots of space, early-opening *Bom Jardim* has tables inside and out, affordable food that kids love, and waiters who are usually extremely child friendly.

The big sights

1 **Torre de Belém** This fabulously ornate tower was built to defend the mouth of the Tejo River and is now the tourist board's icon for Lisbon. **> p.94**

2 **Mosteiro dos Jerónimos** Packed with flamboyant Manueline architectural features, this sixteenth-century monastery commemorates Vasco da Gama's discovery of a sea route to India. > **p.91**

3 **Castelo de São Jorge** Once a Moorish castle and later a palace and prison, the *castelo* is now one of Lisbon's best viewpoints. > **p.48**

4 **Alfama** A maze of steps and tortuous alleys where life continues much as it has for centuries. > **p.51**

5 **Oceanário** A spectacular oceanarium, with a massive high-tech central tank containing everything from sea otters to sharks. > **p.112**

15

Museums and galleries

1 Museu Calouste Gulbenkian Virtually an A–Z of the history of art, from the Mesopotamians to the Impressionists, all set in a delightful park. > **p.103**

2 Berardo Collection See work by some of the biggest names in modern art from Bacon to Rothko, amassed by wealthy Madeiran Joe Berardo. **> p.93**

3 Museu da Marinha A giant overview of the Portuguese maritime explorations, battles and boats from replicas to full-size galleons. **> p.92**

4 Museu Nacional de Arte Antiga Portugal's national gallery includes works by the likes of Nuno Gonçalves and Hieronymus Bosch. **> p.80**

5 Casa das Histórias Cascais' museum building is every bit as stunning as its works of art by vibrant Portuguese contemporary artist Paula Rego. **> p.128**

Eating out

1 Cervejaria da Trindade The nineteenth-century beer hall is touristy but appealing, with decorative tiles, a little garden and tasty seafood. **> p.73**

2 Ribadouro
Bustling restaurant specializing in superb grilled prawns, though other dishes are equally tasty. > **p.109**

3 Mini Bar Theatrical creative cuisine from the country's hippest chef. > **p.63**

4 Bom Jardim, Rei dos Frangos
Not exactly glamorous but the best place in town for delicious barbecue-grilled chicken. > **p.41**

5 Chapitô Buzzing tapas bar-restaurant with one of the best views in the city from its outdoor terrace. > **p.56**

Nightlife

1 Lux Part-owned by John Malkovich and attracting international DJs, this is Lisbon's top club – it also boasts a beautiful rooftop terrace. > **p.57**

2 **Pink Street** This is the place to be seen, filled with clubs, hip bars and fado joints. > **p.61**

4 **A Ginginha** Tiny bar serving *ginginha* (cherry brandy) since 1840: order it with or without the stone to kick-start an evening out. > **p.43**

3 **Chafariz do Vinho Enoteca** This hidden wine bar has cool stone rooms in a cavernous former bathhouse > **p 75**

5 **Portas Largas** Ancient *tasca* (tavern) with original marble counter and tables, but a distinctly modern clientele often spilling out onto the street. > **p.76**

Cafés

1 **Antiga Confeitaria de Belém** This cavernous place serves the best *pastéis de nata* in town – get there early to beat the queues. **> p.97**

2 Confeitaria Nacional Dating from 1829, this small coffee shop is an ornate Baixa classic. > **p.43**

3 Versailles Wonderful café with waiters in bow ties and a fleet of coiffured women devouring cakes and sandwiches > **p.109**

4 A Brasileira The city's most famous café, opened in 1905 and the hub of café society ever since. > **p.64**

5 Pois Café Homely, high-ceilinged café in the heart of Alfama, serving fresh food, cakes and healthy snacks and with comfy sofas to lounge on. > **p.56**

Shopping

1 Mercado da Ribeira Pungent and colourful food market, with fruit, fish and stalls selling drink and tasty food. **> p.60**

2 Armazéns do Chiado Central Lisbon's most appealing shopping centre, with top-floor cafés offering fine city views. > **p.62**

4 Embaixada Various boutiques in this ornate pseudo-Moorish palace are great for a browse. > **p.72**

3 Manuel Tavares This traditional Baixa shop is a great place to buy port wine, local cheese and confectionery. > **p.40**

5 Solar Albuquerque You could spend hours browsing the ceramics, tiles and antiques at this shop specializing in reclaimed items from old houses. > **p.72**

Parks and gardens

1 Jardim Botânico Ancient trees and plants from Portugal's former colonies vie for space in these hidden gardens. **> p.71**

2 Jardim da Estrela A serene space with towering palms and a small lake in an attractive Lisbon suburb. > **p.78**

3 Parque Eduardo VII The views from the top of Lisbon's main park are the main draw, together with the Estufa hothouses. > **p.104**

4 Fundaçao Calouse Gulbenkian Sculptures, walkways and water features puncuate the attractive gardens around this cultural centre, with its own modern amphitheatre. > **p.102**

5 Praça do Império, Belém Lawns edged with topiary, fountains and flowerbeds make up much of Belém's main square, ideal for lounging on a hot summer's day. > **p.90**

Squares

1 Praça do Comércio The city's grandest square, beautifully arcaded and facing the Tagus. **> p.32**

2 Praça do Príncipe Real Filled with ancient trees and fringed by historic mansions, this handsome square hides an intriguing underground reservoir. > **p.70**

3 Praça do Império, Belém This wide-open space by the Tagus is surrounded by some of Belém's grandest buildings. > **p.90**

4 Praça das Amoreiras Edged by a towering aqueduct, Praça das Amoreiras has a laidback, local vibe, with a kiosk café and a children's play area. > **p.99**

5 Largo da Carmo Seats spill out onto this sleepy square where you can find the fascinating Convento do Carmo. > **p.67**

1. THE BAIXA AND ROSSIO > p.32
The heart of the modern city, an elegant grid of eighteenth-century streets running down to the River Tejo.

2. THE SÉ, CASTELO AND ALFAMA > p.44
Next to the Sé cathedral, Alfama is an ancient warren of steep streets leading up to the city's stunning Moorish castle.

3. CHIADO AND CAIS DO SODRÉ > p.58
Lisbon's upscale shopping area, Chiado, rubs shoulders with down-to-earth Cais do Sodré, site of the main market.

4. BAIRRO ALTO AND SAO BENTO > p.66
The Bairro Alto, or Upper Town, shelters the city's best restaurants, bars and clubs, a short walk from the parliament building at São Bento.

5. ESTRELA, LAPA AND SANTOS > p.78
Well-to-do Estrela and Lapa boast gardens and excellent museums, while earthy Santos is the riverside district of design.

6. ALCÂNTARA AND THE DOCKS > p.84
Lisbon's docks shelter appealing riverside bars, clubs, restaurants and a couple of top museums.

7. BELÉM AND AJUDA > p.90
Many of Portugal's maritime explorers set sail from Belém, home to some of the city's finest monuments and museums.

8. AVENIDA, PARQUE EDUARDO VII AND THE GULBENKIAN > p.98
The grand Avenida da Liberdade leads to the leafy Parque Eduardo VII; beyond, the Gulbenkian displays an extraordinarily rich collection of ancient and modern art.

9. PARQUE DAS NAÇÕES > p.110
This futuristic park occupies the former Expo '98 site, with a range of modern attractions including a huge oceanarium.

10. SINTRA > p.116
With its fairy-tale palaces, the hilltop town of Sintra is a must-see day-trip from the capital.

11. THE LISBON COAST > p.126
In less than an hour you can reach superb beaches at Estoril, Cascais or south to Caparica, famed for its surf and miles of sands.

PLACES

The Baixa and Rossio

The tall, imposing buildings that make up the Baixa (Lower Town, pronounced bye-sha) house some of Lisbon's most interesting shops. With around 40 hotels and guesthouses, this is also the tourist epicentre, whose needs are served by a range of cafés, restaurants and street entertainers. Facing the river, this area felt the full force of the 1755 earthquake that destroyed much of what was then one of Europe's wealthiest capitals. The king's minister, the Marquês de Pombal, swiftly redesigned the sector with the grid pattern evident today, framed by a triangle of broad squares. Praça do Comércio sits to the south, with Praça da Figueira and Rossio to the north, the latter having been the city's main square since medieval times.

PRAÇA DO COMÉRCIO

MAP P.33, POCKET MAP E13

The beautiful, arcaded Praça do Comércio represents the climax of Pombal's design. Its classical buildings were once a royal palace and the square is centred on an exuberant bronze equestrian statue of Dom José, monarch during the earthquake and the period of the capital's rebuilding. Two of Portugal's last royals came to a sticky end in this square: in 1908 King Carlos I and his eldest son were shot dead here, clearing the way for the declaration of the Republic two years later.

The square has been partly pedestrianized in recent years in a successful attempt to make it more tourist-friendly, with a panoply of cafés and shops on either side. The secluded Patio da Galé, tucked into the western arcades, hosts frequent events, including the alluring Lisbon Fish Festival in April. The north side of the square is where you can start tram tours of the city. However, it is the square's riverfront that is perhaps most appealing, especially in the hour or two before sunset, when people linger in the golden light to watch the orange ferries ply between the Estação Fluvial ferry station and Barreiro on the other side of the Tejo. An attractive walk is to head west along the pedestrianized riverfront to Cais do Sodré (see p.52).

ARCADE ON PRAÇA DO COMÉRCIO

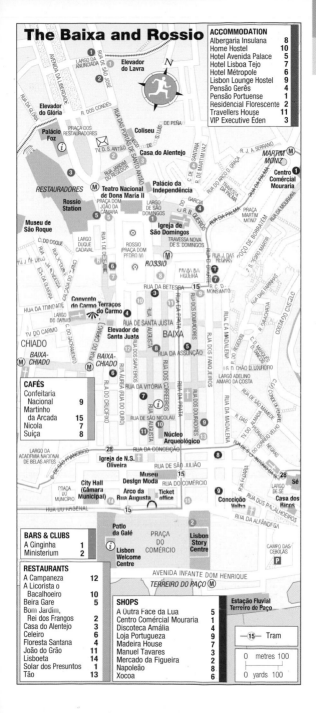

The Baixa and Rossio

ACCOMMODATION

Albergaria Insulana	8
Home Hostel	10
Hotel Avenida Palace	5
Hotel Lisboa Tejo	7
Hotel Métropole	6
Lisbon Lounge Hostel	9
Pensão Gerês	4
Pensão Portuense	1
Residencial Florescente	2
Travellers House	11
VIP Executive Éden	3

CAFÉS

Confeitaria Nacional	9
Martinho da Arcada	15
Nicola	7
Suíça	8

BARS & CLUBS

A Ginginha	1
Ministerium	2

RESTAURANTS

A Campaneza	12
A Licorista o Bacalhoeiro	10
Beira Gare	5
Bom Jardim, Rei dos Frangos	2
Casa do Alentejo	3
Celeiro	6
Floresta Santana	4
João do Grão	11
Lisboeta	14
Solar dos Presuntos	1
Tão	13

SHOPS

A Outra Face da Lua	5
Centro Comércial Mouraria	1
Discoteca Amália	4
Loja Portugueza	9
Madeira House	7
Manuel Tavares	3
Mercado da Figueira	2
Napoleão	8
Xocoa	6

15 — Tram

0   metres   100
0   yards   100

LISBON STORY CENTRE

Praça do Comércio 78–81 ⓜ Terreiro de Paço ☎ 211 941 099, ⓦ www.lisboa storycentre.pt. Daily 10am–8pm. €7 (ticket valid for one year). MAP P.33, POCKET MAP E13

This is the highlight of a group of touristy cafés and shops that fill the square's historic eastern arcades. The Centre gives a potted, visual account of the city's history – good for a rainy day, though somewhat pricey. There are six zones, each dedicated to a phase in Lisbon's past. The multimedia displays include models, paintings, photos, narrations and filmed re-enactments – the highlight is a somewhat gory 4D film depicting the 1755 earthquake, and a "virtual" scale model of the modern city.

ARCO DA RUA AUGUSTA

ⓜ Terreiro de Paço ⓦ www.visitlisboa.com. Daily: 9am–7pm. €2.50. MAP P.33, POCKET MAP E13

Praça do Comércio's most prominent building is a huge arch, the Arco da Rua Augusta, adorned with statues of historical figures, including the Marquês de Pombal and Vasco da Gama. Acting as a gateway to the city, the arch was built to celebrate Lisbon's reconstruction after the earthquake, although it wasn't completed until 1873. You can take a lift up the structure to just below the Clock Room, a small exhibition space centred round the workings of a nineteenth-century clock. From here, you can squeeze up a spiral staircase to the flat roof of the monument where you'll be greeted by unmissable views across the Praça do Comércio and the Baixa. Don't be tempted to stand under the bell here. When it strikes, you'll regret it.

ALEXANDER MCQUEEN SKIRT, MUSEU DESIGN MODA

RUA AUGUSTA

POCKET MAP D11

Completely paved in mosaics, the broad Rua Augusta runs from Praça do Comércio up to Rossio and is the Baixa's main pedestrianized thoroughfare. Filled with shops, market stalls and touristy restaurants, it can get pretty packed, but its buskers and street performers are always entertaining.

MUSEU DESIGN MODA

Rua Augusta 24 ☎ 218 886 117, ⓦ www.mude .pt. Tues–Sun 10am–6pm. Free. MAP P.33, POCKET MAP E13

Housed in a grand former bank, the Museu Design Moda (closed for renovation till the end of 2017) is an impressive collection of design and fashion classics from the 1930s to today amassed by former stockbroker and media mogul Francisco Capelo. The museum's ever-changing exhibitions include design classics, such as furniture by Charles and Ray Eames and Phillipe Starck, and also features Capelo's fashion collection – haute couture from the 1950s, 1960s street fashion and the brand labelling of the 1990s. Look out for Ron Arad's "Big

The Lisbon Earthquake

Early eighteenth-century Lisbon had been one of the most active and important ports in Europe, making the Great Earthquake of 1755 all the more tragic. The quake, which was felt as far away as Jamaica, struck Lisbon at 9.30am on November 1 (All Saints' Day), when most of the city's population was at Mass. Within the space of ten minutes there had been three major tremors and the candles of a hundred church altars had started fires that raged throughout the capital. A vast tidal wave later swept the waterfront and, in all, 40,000 of the 270,000 population died. The destruction of the city shocked the continent and prompted religious debate between philosophers Voltaire and Rousseau. For Portugal, it was a disaster that ended its capital's golden age.

Easy" steel chair (1951), Frank Gehry's wiggle chair (1972) and the 1959 Vespa, while fashionistas will adore Paco Rabanne's metalized leather boots, Pierre Cardin's 1950s coats and Alexander McQueen's superb fur skirt. There's also a bookshop and café.

PRAÇA DO MUNICÍPIO

MAP P.33, POCKET MAP D13

The attractive, mosaic-paved Praça do Município houses the Neoclassical nineteenth-century Câmara Municipal (City Hall), where the Portuguese Republic was declared in 1910, flatteringly described by Portugal's greatest twentieth-century poet as "one of the finest buildings in the city". The square adjoins Rua do Arsenal, an atmospheric street lined with pungent shops selling dried cod and grocers selling cheap wines, port and brandy.

THE BAIXA GRID

MAP P.33, POCKET MAP D11-12

Pombal designed the Baixa to have three main streets dissected by nine smaller streets. Many of these streets took their names from the crafts and businesses carried out there, like Rua da Prata (Silversmiths' Street) and Rua dos Sapateiros (Cobblers' Street). Modern banks and shops have disturbed these divisions somewhat, though plenty of traditional stores remain; the central section of Rua da Conceição, for example, is still lined with shops selling beads and sequins. Some of the most interesting streets to explore are the smaller ones running south to north – Rua dos Correeiros, Rua dos Douradores and Rua dos Sapateiros. Pombal also wanted the grid's churches to blend in with his harmonious design, so much so that they are almost invisible – walk along Rua de São Julião and the facade of the church of Oliveira is barely distinguishable from the offices alongside it, though its tiled interior is delightful.

THE BAIXA GRID

Fernando Pessoa

Martinho da Arcada, the café at the north end of Praça do Comércio, was the favoured haunt of Fernando Pessoa (1888–1935), Portugal's greatest contemporary poet and a leading figure of twentieth-century modernism. Born in Lisbon, Pessoa grew up in South Africa before returning to Portugal in 1905 to work as a translator. He spent much of his time composing poems in Lisbon's cafés. Many of his works are about identity – he wrote under various alter egos or "heteronyms", each with their own personality and style. The most famous are Alberto Caeiro, Ricardo Reis and Alvaro de Campos, though his most famous work is the *Book of Disquiet* written under the heteronym Bernardo Soares. The partly autobiographical work is full of extraordinary philosophical ruminations that have established his reputation as a leading existentialist artist.

NÚCLEO ARQUEOLÓGICO

Rua dos Correeiros 9 ☎ 211 131 004. ⓦ ind .millenniumbcp.pt. Advance bookings required. Mon–Sat 10am–noon & 2–5pm. Free. MAP P.33, POCKET MAP E12

One of Lisbon's smallest but most fascinating museums lies beneath the Baixa's streets. The remains of Roman fish-preserving tanks, a fifth-century Christian burial place and Moorish ceramics can all be seen in the tiny Núcleo Arqueológico, containing the remains of excavations revealed during building work on the BCP bank. Most exhibits are viewed through glass floors or from cramped walkways under the modern bank during a 60-minute tour. Pombal actually rebuilt most of the Baixa on a riverbed, and you can even see the wooden piles driven into the water-logged soil to support the buildings, the same device that is used in Venice.

If you're interested in discovering more about Lisbon's underground ruins, ask the museum about early summer visits to the amazing Roman tunnels that lie beneath the Baixa. Access is restricted to the 2000-year-old tunnels, whose purpose remains unclear, because they are usually flooded. As a result they are open for just three days a year and attract enormous queues. It's a bizarre sight watching people enter the tunnels, which can only be accessed through a manhole cover between tram tracks on Rua da Conceição.

ELEVADOR DE SANTA JUSTA

PRAÇA DOM PEDRO IV

ELEVADOR DE SANTA JUSTA

Rua do Santa Justa. Daily: Oct–May
7am–9.45pm; June–Sept 7am–11pm. €5
return. MAP P.33, POCKET MAP D11

Raul Mésnier's extraordinary
and eccentric Elevador de
Santa Justa was built in 1902 by
a disciple of Eiffel. Its giant lift
whisks you 32m up the inside
of a latticework metal tower, to
deposit you on a platform high
above the Baixa. Before taking
the upper exit on to the Largo
do Carmo (see p.67), head up
the dizzy spiral staircase to the
pricey rooftop café with great
views over the city.

ROSSIO

MAP P.33, POCKET MAP C11

Praça Dom Pedro IV
(popularly known as Rossio)
has been the city's main square
since medieval times and it
remains the hub of commercial
Lisbon. Its central space
sparkles with Baroque
fountains and polished,
mosaic-cobbled pavements.
During the nineteenth century,
Rossio's plethora of cafés
attracted Lisbon's painters and
writers, though many of the
artists' haunts were converted
to banks in the 1970s.
Nevertheless, the outdoor seats
of the square's remaining cafés
are perennially popular
meeting points. On the
northwestern side of the
square, there's a horseshoe-
shaped entrance to Rossio
station, a mock-Manueline
complex with the train
platforms an escalator ride
above the street-level entrances.

TEATRO NACIONAL DE DONA MARIA II

Rossio ☎ 213 250 800, 🌐 www.teatro-dmaria
.pt. MAP P.33, POCKET MAP D10

Rossio's biggest concession to
grandeur is the Teatro Nacional
de Dona Maria II built along its
north side in the 1840s, and
heavily restored after a fire in
1964. Inside there is a good
café. Prior to the earthquake,
the Inquisitional Palace stood
on this site, in front of which
public hangings and autos-da-
fé (ritual burnings of heretics)
took place.

IGREJA DE SÃO DOMINGOS

Largo de São Domingos ☎ 213 428 275.
Daily: 7.30am–7pm. MAP P.33, POCKET MAP D11

The Igreja de São Domingos
stands on the site of the
thirteenth-century Convento
de São Domingos, where
sentences were read out during
the Inquisition. The convent
was destroyed in the earthquake of 1755, though its
portal was reconstructed soon
after as part of the current
Dominican church. For over a
century it was the venue for
royal marriages and christen-
ings, though it lost this role
after the declaration of the
Republic and was then gutted
by a fire in the 1950s. Some say
the fire purged some unsavoury
acts that took place on the spot,
such as the massacre of forcibly
converted Jews (known as
"New Christians") which began
here in 1506. It was reopened
in 1997 after partial restoration
to replace the seats and some
statues; however, the rest of the
cavernous interior and the
scarred pillars remain
powerfully atmospheric.

PRAÇA DA FIGUEIRA

MAP P.33, POCKET MAP D11

Praça da Figueira is a historic
square (once the site of Lisbon's
main market), though the
recent addition of an
underground car park has
detracted from its former
grandeur. Nevertheless, it is
slightly quieter than Rossio,
and its cafés offer appealing
views of the green slopes of the
Castelo de São Jorge.

PRAÇA DOS RESTAURADORES

MAP P.33, POCKET MAP C10

The elongated Praça dos
Restauradores (Square of the
Restorers) takes its name from
the renewal of independence
from Spain in 1640. To the
north of the square, the
Elevador da Glória offers
access to the Bairro Alto (see
p.66); south sits the superb Art
Deco frontage of the old Eden
cinema, now an apartment-
hotel (see p.135). The square is
dominated by the pink Palácio
de Foz on the western side,
which housed the Ministry of
Propaganda under the Salazar

PRAÇA DOS RESTAURADORES

CASA DO ALENTEJO

regime (1932–74) but is now home to the Portuguese Tourist Office (see p.149) and tourist police station. During the week it is sometimes possible to visit the palace's ornate upper floors (enquire at the tourist office).

RUA DAS PORTAS DE SANTO ANTÃO

MAP P.33, POCKET MAP D10

The pedestrianized Rua das Portas de Santo Antão is well known for its seafood restaurants. Despite the tourist trappings – this and the adjacent Rua Jardim Regedor are the only places in town you're likely to get waiters trying to smooth-talk you into their premises – it is worth eating here at least once to sample its seafood. The street is also home to several theatres, and the domed **Coliseu dos Recreios** at #96 (☎ 213 240 580, ⓦ www.coliseulisboa.com), which opened in 1890 as a circus but is now one of Lisbon's main concert venues.

CASA DO ALENTEJO

Rua de Santo Antão 58 Ⓜ Terreiro de Paço ☎ 213 469 231, ⓦ www.casadoalentejo .pt. Daily 10am–10pm. Free. MAP P.33, POCKET MAP D10

A cultural centre with its own café-bar and restaurant (see p.41), the Casa do Alentejo is a sumptuously decorated pseudo-Moorish palace, little changed for decades. Originally a seventeenth-century mansion and later a casino, it has been a centre dedicated to culture from the Alentejo district since the 1930s. You can just wander in and look around the beautifully tiled interior – some of the tiles are from the original mansion – but most visitors head upstairs to the dining room or café-bar, with its neighbouring ballroom, an amazing, slightly rundown room hung with chandeliers.

ELEVADOR DO LAVRA

Largo da Anunciada. Mon–Fri 7.50am–7.55pm, Sat & Sun 9am–7.55pm. €3.60 return. MAP P.33, POCKET MAP K5

Rua das Portas de Santo Antão ends next to where another of the city's classic *elevadores*, Elevador do Lavra, begins its ascent. The funicular opened in 1884 and is Lisbon's oldest and least tourist-frequented *elevador*. At the top a short walk down Travessa do Torel takes you to **Jardim do Torel**, a tiny park offering exhilarating views over the city.

Shops

A OUTRA FACE DA LUA

Rua da Assunção 22. Mon–Sat 10am–8pm,
Sun noon–7pm. MAP P.33, POCKET MAP E12

This buzzy space specializes in
retro fashion – fab vintage
clothes, tin toys and the like;
it also has a great attached café
serving *crostini* and snacks.

CENTRO COMÉRCIAL MOURARIA

Largo Martim Moniz. Most shops Mon–Sat
9am–8pm. MAP P.33, POCKET MAP E10

A shopping centre with
hundreds of small, family-run
stores selling Indian fabrics and
oriental and African produce,
alongside an aromatic
collection of cafés on Level –3,
which give an insight into
Lisbon's ethnic communities,
perfect if you need an Afro
haircut or a sari.

DISCOTECA AMÁLIA

Rua Áurea 272. Mon–Sat 9am–7pm. MAP P.33,
POCKET MAP D11

A small but well-stocked shop
named after famous fado singer
Amália Rodrigues, with a good
collection of traditional
Portuguese fado music. If
you're looking for a recommendation, the English-speaking
staff are usually happy to help.

LOJA PORTUGUEZA

Rua da Fanqueiros 32. Daily 10am–7pm. MAP
P.33, POCKET MAP E13

A packed treasure-trove of
Portuguese crafts and
souvenirs, including tasteful
mugs, tiles, port and trinkets.

MADEIRA HOUSE

Rua Augusta 133. Daily 9am–9pm, Sat & Sun
closed from 1–3pm. MAP P.33, POCKET MAP D12

As you'd expect, linens and
embroidery from Madeira
feature, along with some
attractive ceramics, tiles and
souvenirs from the mainland.

MERCADO PRAÇA DA FIGUEIRA

MANUEL TAVARES

Rua da Betesga 1a. Mon–Sat
9.30am–7.30pm. MAP P.33, POCKET MAP D11

Small treasure-trove dating
from 1860, with a great
selection of nuts, chocolate and
national cheeses, and a
basement stuffed with vintage
wines and ports, some dating
from the early 1900s.

MERCADO DA FIGUEIRA

Praça da Figueira 10b. Mon–Fri 8.30am–8pm,
Sat 8.30am–7pm. MAP P.33, POCKET MAP E11

The decorative, narrow
entrance hall gives onto a
well-stocked supermarket with
a good array of inexpensive
wines, ports and fresh produce
and its own café.

NAPOLEÃO

Rua dos Fanqueiros 68–70. Mon–Sat 9.30am–
8pm, Sun 1–8pm. MAP P.33, POCKET MAP E12

This spruce shop offers a great
range of quality port and wine
from all Portugal's main
regions, and its enthusiastic
English-speaking staff can
advise on what to buy.

XOCOA

Rua do Crucifixo 112–114 ☎ 213 466 370.
Mon–Sat 10am–8pm. MAP P.33, POCKET MAP D12

Chocolate shops are a relative rarity in Portugal so this Spanish shop has become all the rage for chocoholics. There's hot chocolate to take away and a staggering variety of chocolate bars, biscuits and cakes.

Restaurants

A CAMPANEZA

Rua dos Sapateiros 155–157. Mon & Thurs–Sun 7–11pm. MAP P.33, POCKET MAP D12

Formerly a *leituria* (dairy shop) and still displaying the Art Nouveau decor from its past existence, this is now a simple restaurant, with a short, moderately priced menu.

A LICORISTA O BACALHOEIRO

Rua dos Sapateiros 222–224 ☎ 213 431 415.
Mon–Sat noon–3pm & 7–10pm. MAP P.33, POCKET MAP D11

This pleasant tile-and-brick restaurant is a popular lunchtime stop, when locals flock in for inexpensive set meals or mains from around €8.

BEIRA GARE

Praça D. João de Câmara 4. Daily 9am–10pm.
MAP P.33, POCKET MAP D11

Well-established café-restaurant opposite Rossio station, serving stand-up Portuguese snacks and bargain meals (mains from €7). Constantly busy, which is recommendation enough.

BOM JARDIM, REI DOS FRANGOS

Trav de Santo Antão 11–18 ☎ 213 424 389.
Daily noon–11.30pm (closed Wed all day and Thurs lunch from Oct–March).
MAP P.33, POCKET MAP C10

A bit of a Lisbon institution thanks to its spit-roast chickens and now so popular that it has spread into three buildings on either side of a pedestrianized alley. There are plenty of tables outdoors, too. A half-chicken is yours for around €8, though it also serves other meat and fish at less generous prices.

CASA DO ALENTEJO

Rua das Portas de Santo Antão 58 ☎ 213 405 150, ⓦ www.casadoalentejo.com.pt.
Daily noon–3pm & 7–10.30pm. MAP P.33, POCKET MAP D10

A centre dedicated to Alentejan culture (see p.39), with its own restaurant, in a beautifully tiled upstairs dining room. Alentejo specialities include oven-roasted rabbit and *carne de porco à alentejana* (grilled pork with clams) with mains from €11; or just pop in for a drink in the superb bar or courtyard taverna.

CASA DO ALENTEJO

A starter for ten euros?

At restaurants, don't feel you're being ripped off when you're served an array of starters before you even order your main course, then get a bill for what you've eaten at the end. This is normal practice in Portugal and no waiter will take offence if you politely decline whatever you're offered. Starters can vary from simple bread, butter and olives to prawns, cheeses and cured meats. If you're tempted, it's a good idea to ask the waiter how much each item costs. Check your bill, too, to ensure you've not been charged for anything you declined.

CELEIRO

Rua 1° de Dezembro 45 ☎ 210 306 030, ⓦ www.celeiro.pt. Mon–Fri 9am–6pm, Sat 9am–5pm. MAP P.33, POCKET MAP D11

Just off Rossio, this inexpensive self-service restaurant sits in the basement of a health-food supermarket and offers tasty vegetarian spring rolls, quiches, pizza and the like from around €6. There's also a streetside café offering snacks and drinks.

FLORESTA SANTANA

Calçada Santana 18 ☎ 963 945 338. Mon–Sat 10am–11pm. MAP P.33, POCKET MAP D10

A short (uphill) walk from the bustle of the Baixa but a world away in terms of atmosphere: excellent-value meals served in a friendly, family-run place which gets busy at lunchtimes. The fish and meat is fresh and generous and desserts are home-made and huge. Two courses with wine come to around €10–15.

JOÃO DO GRÃO

Rua dos Correeiros 222–226 ☎ 213 424 757. Daily noon–3.30pm & 6–10pm. MAP P.33, POCKET MAP D11

One of the best in a row of restaurants on this pedestrianized street, where appealing outdoor tables tempt you to sample the reasonably priced salads, fish and rice dishes (from €9). The marble- and azulejo-clad interior is just as attractive.

LISBOETA

Praça do Comércio 31–34 ☎ 210 407 641, ⓦ www.pousadas.pt. Daily 1–3pm & 7.30–10pm. MAP P.33, POCKET MAP D13

Inside Lisbon Pousada, formerly the Ministry for Internal Affairs, the smart but casual Restaurante Lisboeta serves top-notch contemporary Portuguese cuisine. Expect the likes of scallops with champagne, Alentejo black pork or aged beef. Mains from €25.

SOLAR DOS PRESUNTOS

Rua das Portas de Santo Antão 150 ☎ 213 424 253. Mon–Sat 12.30–3.30pm & 7–11pm. MAP P.33, POCKET MAP J5

The "Manor House of Hams" is, not surprisingly, best known for its smoked ham from the Minho region in northern Portugal, served cold as a starter. There are also excellent, if expensive, meat and seafood dishes, many using traditional recipes. Popular with celebrities; it's best to book a table.

TÃO

Rua dos Douradores 10 ☎ 218 850 046. Tues–Sat noon–4pm & 6.30–9.30pm, Mon noon–4pm. MAP P.33, POCKET MAP E12

Fashionable, very good value Eastern-inspired organic restaurant, with set buffet meals from around €7. Tasty vegetarian sushi, risottos, grilled aubergines and salads.

Cafés

CONFEITARIA NACIONAL

Praça da Figueira 18. Daily 8am–8pm.
MAP P.33, POCKET MAP D11

Opened in 1829 and little changed since, with a stand-up counter selling pastries and sweets below mirrors and stucco ceilings. There's a little side room and outdoor seating for sit-down coffees and snacks.

MARTINHO DA ARCADA

Praça do Comércio 3. Mon–Sat 7am–11pm.
MAP P.33, POCKET MAP E13

One of Lisbon's oldest café restaurante, first opened in 1782 and declared a national monument in 1910. It has been a gambling den, a meeting place for political dissidents and, later, a more reputable hangout for politicians, writers and artists. It is now divided into a simple stand-up café and a slightly pricey restaurant. The outdoor tables under the arches are a perfect spot for a coffee and a *pastel de nata*.

NICOLA

Rossio 24–25. Daily 8am–midnight. MAP P.33, POCKET MAP D11

The only surviving Rossio coffee house from the nineteenth century, once the haunt of some of Lisbon's great literary figures. The outdoor tables overlooking the bustle of Rossio are the best feature, though it has sacrificed much of its period interior in the name of modernization. Also has live fado from Thursday to Saturday at 8.30pm.

SUÍÇA

Rossio 96–104. Daily 7am–9pm. MAP P.33, POCKET MAP D11

Founded in 1922, this is famous for its cakes and pastries; you'll have a hard job getting an outdoor table here,

MARTINHO DA ARCADA

though there's plenty of room inside. There's more alfresco seating in Praça da Figueira.

Bars

A GINGINHA

Largo de São Domingos 8. Daily 9am–10pm.
MAP P.33, POCKET MAP D11

Everyone should try *ginginha* – Portuguese cherry brandy – once. There's just about room in this microscopic joint to walk in, down a glassful and stagger outside to see the city in a new light.

MINISTERIUM CLUB

Ala Nascente 72, Praça do Comércio ☎916 931 884, ⓦ www.ministerium.pt. Sat 11pm–6am. MAP P.33, POCKET MAP E13

The grand and historic buildings of the former Ministry of Finance partly make up the stylish backdrop to this hip club mostly playing house and techno and attracting top-name DJs. There's a spacious dancefloor plus quieter zones and a great rooftop café-bar if you get the munchies.

The Sé, Castelo and Alfama

East of the Baixa, the streets climb past the city's ancient cathedral, or Sé, to the dramatic remains of the Castelo de São Jorge, an oasis of tranquillity high above the city. East of the castle lie two of Lisbon's most prominent churches, São Vicente de Fora and Santa Engrácia. The districts around the castle – Mouraria, Santa Cruz and particularly the Alfama – represent the oldest and most atmospheric parts of Lisbon. Down on the riverfront, Santa Apolónia, the international train station, is situated in a revitalized area that boasts the glitzy *Lux* club and cruise ship terminal, while a little further east lies a historic steam pumping station and a fascinating tile museum.

THE SÉ

Largo da Sé ☎ 218 876 628. Daily 9am–7pm. Free. Tram #28. MAP PP.46–47. POCKET MAP F12

Lisbon's main cathedral, the Sé, was founded in 1150 to commemorate the city's Reconquest from the Moors on the site of their main mosque. It's a Romanesque structure with a suitably fortress-like appearance. The great rose window and twin towers form a simple and effective facade, although there's nothing particularly exciting inside: the building was once splendidly embellished on the orders of Dom João V, but his Rococo whims were swept away by the 1755 earthquake and subsequent restorers. All that remains is a group of Gothic tombs behind the high altar and the decaying thirteenth-century **cloister** (daily 10am–6.30pm; Oct–April closes 5.30pm; €2.50). This has been heavily excavated, revealing the remains of a sixth-century Roman house and Moorish public buildings.

The Baroque **Treasury** (Mon–Sat 10am–5pm; €2.50) holds a small museum of treasures including the relics of St Vincent, brought to Lisbon in 1173 in a boat that was piloted by ravens,

THE SÉ CATHEDRAL

according to legend. Ravens were kept in the cloisters for centuries afterwards, but the tradition halted when the last one died in 1978. To this day, the birds remain one of the city's symbols.

IGREJA DE SANTO ANTÓNIO AND MUSEU ANTONIANO

Largo S. António da Sé ☎ 218 860 447. Tram #28. MAP PP.46–47, POCKET MAP E12

The small eighteenth-century church of **Santo António** (open daily) is said to have been built on the spot where the city's most popular saint was born as Fernando Bulhões; after his death in Italy in 1231 he became known as St Anthony of Padua. The tiny neighbouring **museum** (Tues–Sun 10am–1pm & 2–6pm; free) chronicles the saint's life, including his enviable skill at fixing marriages, though only devotees will find interest in the statues and endless images.

CASA DOS BICOS

Rua dos Bacalhoeiros 10 ☎ 218 802 040. Ⓦ www.josesaramago.org. Mon–Sat 10am–6pm. €3 (archeological area free). MAP PP.46–47, POCKET MAP F13

The Casa dos Bicos means the "House of Points", and its curious walls – set with diamond-shaped stones – give an idea of the richness of pre-1755 Lisbon. It was built in 1523 for the son of the Viceroy of India, though only the lower facade of the original building survived the earthquake. It is now owned by the Saramargo organization which uses the venue for recitals and exhibitions dedicated to the Nobel Prize for Literature winning Portuguese author José Saramago, who died in 2010.

The ground floor has been maintained as an archeological area where you can view sections of a third-century Roman wall and fish-processing plant, excavated from beneath the building.

Lisbon graffiti

Art or vandalism? In Lisbon, like anywhere else, the merits of graffiti splits opinions, but the balance generally tips towards the former, largely thanks to the far-sightedness of the council. Realizing that graffiti has long been a feature of Lisbon life – once in the form of political protest under the Salazar regime – the council's heritage department has given over certain city walls to be part of a Galeria de Arte Urbana, in which street art is positively encouraged. There is even an organization, Lata65, which runs workshops in street art for the over-65s, while an annual urban art festival, O Bairro i o Mundo, has been credited with alleviating some of the problems of the tough Quinta do Mocho district north of the airport. The result is a dazzling array of graffiti all over the city. Lisbon's best-known graffiti artist is Alexandre Farto, aka Vhils, whose large and striking works are often chiselled into brickwork using pneumatic drills. You can see some of his work near the docks opposite the Alfama and alongside Santa Apolónia station.

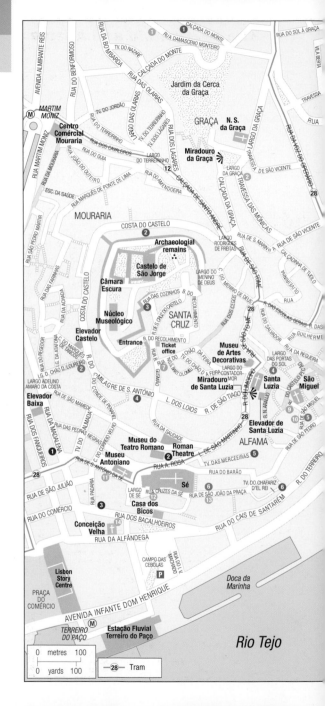

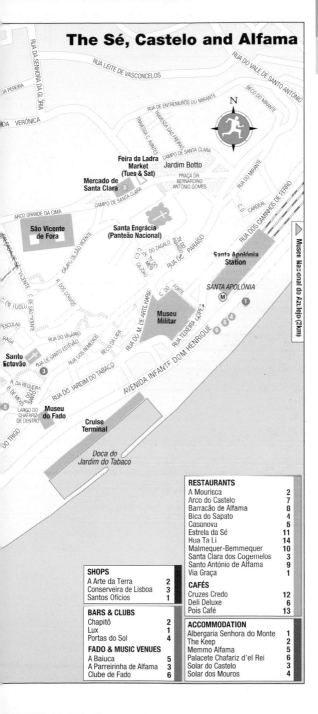

The Sé, Castelo and Alfama

Museu Nacional do Azulejo (2km)

RESTAURANTS

A Mourisca	2
Arco do Castelo	7
Barracão de Alfama	8
Bica do Sapato	4
Casanova	5
Estrela da Sé	11
Hua Ta Li	14
Malmequer-Bemmequer	10
Santa Clara dos Cogemelos	3
Santo António de Alfama	9
Via Graça	1

CAFÉS

Cruzes Credo	12
Deli Deluxe	6
Pois Café	13

SHOPS

A Arte da Terra	2
Conserveira de Lisboa	3
Santos Ofícios	1

BARS & CLUBS

Chapitô	2
Lux	1
Portas do Sol	4

FADO & MUSIC VENUES

A Baiuca	5
A Parreirinha de Alfama	3
Clube de Fado	6

ACCOMMODATION

Albergaria Senhora do Monte	1
The Keep	2
Memmo Alfama	5
Palacete Chafariz d'el Rei	6
Solar do Castelo	3
Solar dos Mouros	4

MUSEU DO TEATRO ROMANO

Entrance on Patio de Aljube 5 ☎ 218 820 320, ⓦ www.museuteatroromano.pt. Tues-Sun 10am-1pm & 2-6pm. Free. Tram #28. MAP PP.46-47, POCKET MAP F12

The Museu do Teatro Romano displays a wealth of Roman coins, spoons and fragments of pots, statues and columns excavated from the ruins of a Roman theatre, dating from 57 AD, which are fenced off just north of Rua Augusto Rosa. Roman Lisbon – Olisipo – became the administrative capital of Lusitania, the western part of Iberia, under Julius Caesar in 60 BC, and the theatre shows the wealth that quickly grew thanks to its fish-preserving industries.

MIRADOURO DE SANTA LUZIA

MAP PP.46-47, POCKET MAP F12

The church of Santa Luzia marks the entry to the Miradouro de Santa Luzia, a spectacular viewpoint where elderly Lisboetas play cards and tourists gather to take in the sweeping views across the Alfama and the river beyond.

MUSEU DE ARTES DECORATIVAS

MUSEU DE ARTES DECORATIVAS

Largo das Portas do Sol 2 ☎ 218 814 600, ⓦ www.fress.pt. Mon & Wed-Sun 10am-5pm. €4. MAP PP.46-47, POCKET MAP F11

Set in the seventeenth-century Azurara Palace, this fascinating museum contains some of the best examples of sixteenth- to eighteenth-century applied art in the country. Founded by a wealthy banker and donated to the nation in 1953, the museum boasts unique pieces of furniture, major collections of gold, silver and porcelain, magnificent paintings and textiles. The rambling building covers five floors, set around a stairway decorated with spectacular *azulejos*. Highlights include a stunning sixteenth-century tapestry depicting a parade of giraffes, beautiful carpets from Arraiolos in the Alentejo district, and oriental-influenced quilts that were all the rage during the seventeenth and eighteenth centuries. The museum also has a small café with a patio garden.

CASTELO DE SÃO JORGE

Bus #37 from Praça da Figueira ☎ 218 800 620, ⓦ www.castelosaojorge.pt. Daily: March-Oct 9am-9pm; Nov-Feb 9am-6pm. €8.50 includes visit to Câmara Escura Núcleo Museológico. MAP PP.46-47, POCKET MAP F11

Reached by a confusing but well-signposted series of twisting roads, the Castelo de São Jorge is perhaps the most spectacular building in Lisbon, as much because of its position as anything else. Now Lisbon's most-visited tourist site, the castle was once the heart of a walled city that spread downhill as far as the river. The original Moorish castle on this site was besieged in 1147 by a particularly ruthless gang of Crusaders who, together with King Alfonso I of Portugal, conquered Lisbon after some four hundred years of Moorish rule. Badly damaged during the seige, its fortifications were rebuilt. From the fourteenth century, Portuguese kings took up residence in the old Moorish palace, or Alcáçova, within the walls, but by the early sixteenth century they had moved to the new royal palace on Praça do Comércio. Subsequently, the castle was used as a prison and then as an army barracks until the 1920s. The walls were partly renovated by Salazar in the 1930s and further restored for Expo '98. A series of gardens, walkways and **viewpoints** hidden within the old Moorish walls makes this an enjoyable place in which to wander about for a couple of hours, with spectacular views over the city from its ramparts and towers.

CASTELO DE SÃO JORGE VIEWPOINT

CÂMARA ESCURA

Castelo de Sao Jorge. Weather permitting, daily 10am–5pm. MAP PP46–47, POCKET MAP F11

One of the castle towers, the Tower of Ulysses, now holds a kind of periscope which projects sights from around the city onto a white disc with commentary in English. Unless you like being holed up in dark chambers with up to fifteen other people, though, you may prefer to see the view in the open air.

NÚCLEO MUSEOLÓGICO AND ARCHEOLOGICAL REMAINS

Castelo de São Jorge. Daily: March–Oct 10am–8pm; Nov–Feb 9am–5.30pm. MAP PP46–47, POCKET MAP F11

Only a much-restored shell remains of the old Moorish Alcáçova. This now houses the Núcleo Museológico, a small museum containing items unearthed during excavations in the castle, including Moorish lamps, Roman storage jars and coins, and pottery and tiles from the seventeenth century. Take time to explore the Archeological Remains, an excavation site that includes the scant remains of an Iron Age house, an eleventh-century Moorish quarter and the ruins of the fifteenth-century Palácio dos Condes de Santiago, built for the Bishops of Lisbon.

SANTA CRUZ AND MOURARIA

MAP PP46–47, POCKET MAP F11

Crammed within the castle's outer walls, but free to enter, is the tiny medieval quarter of Santa Cruz. This remains a village in its own right, with its own school, bathhouse and church. Leaving Santa Cruz, a tiny arch at the end of Rua do Chão da Feira leads through to Rua dos Cegos and down to Largo Rodrigues de Freitas, which marks the eastern edge of Mouraria, the district to which the Moors were relegated after the siege of Lisbon – hence the name. Today Mouraria is an atmospheric residential area.

SÃO VICENTE DE FORA

MIRADOURO DA GRAÇA

MAP PP.46-47, POCKET MAP F10

The Miradouro da Graça provides superb views over Lisbon and the castle. To reach it take tram #28 (see p.53) to the broad Largo da Graça. From here, head past Nossa Senhora da Graça – a church which partly dates from 1271, making it one of the oldest in the city – to the viewpoint which also has a small kiosk café-bar. Below the *miradouro*, steps lead down to the Jardim da Cerca da Graça, Lisbon's newest park, which opened in 2015. There's a children's play area, lawns and appealing walkways.

SÃO VICENTE DE FORA

Largo de São Vicente ☎ 218 810 559. Tues–Sun 10am–6pm. Church free, monastery €5. Tram #28. MAP PP.46-47, POCKET MAP G11

The church of São Vicente de Fora stands as a reminder of the extent of the sixteenth-century city; its name means "Saint Vincent of the Outside". It was built during the years of Spanish rule by Philip II's Italian architect, Felipe Terzi (1582–1629); its geometric facade was

an important Renaissance innovation. Of more interest is the adjoining monastery. Through the beautiful cloisters, decorated with *azulejos* representing scenes from Portugal's history, you can visit the old monastic refectory, which since 1855 has formed the pantheon of the Bragança dynasty. Here, in more or less complete sequence, are the **tombs** of all the Portuguese kings from João IV, who restored the monarchy in 1640, to Manuel II, the last Portuguese monarch who died in exile in England in 1932. Among them is Catherine of Bragança, the widow of England's Charles II, who is credited with introducing the concept of "teatime" to the British. If you have energy, climb to the roof for spectacular views out over the city. There's also a lovely café by the entrance if you do fancy a cup of tea.

FEIRA DA LADRA

Campo de Santa Clara. Tues and Sat 9am–around 3pm. Tram #28. MAP PP.46-47, POCKET MAP H10

The leafy square of Campo de Santa Clara is home to the twice-weekly Feira da Ladra

("Thieves' Market"), Lisbon's main flea market. It's not the world's greatest market, but it does turn up some interesting things, like oddities from the former African colonies and old Portuguese prints. Out-and-out junk – from broken alarm clocks to old postcards – is spread on the ground above Santa Engrácia, with cheap clothes, CDs and half-genuine antiques at the top end of the *feira*. The covered *mercado* (market) building has a fine array of fresh fruit and vegetables.

SANTA ENGRÁCIA

Campo de Santa Clara ☎ 218 854 820. Tues–Sun: May–Oct 10am–6pm; Nov–April 10am–5pm. €3.50. Tram #28. MAP PP.46–47, POCKET MAP H10

The white dome of Santa Engrácia makes it the loftiest church in the city, and it has become synonymous with unfinished work – begun in 1682, it was only completed in 1966. It is now the **Panteão Nacional**, housing the tombs of eminent Portuguese figures, including writer Almeida Garrett (1799–1854) and Amália Rodrigues (1920–99),

Portugal's most famous fado singer, and football legend Eusébio. You can take the stairs up to the terrace, from where there are great views over eastern Lisbon.

THE ALFAMA

MAP PP.46–47, POCKET MAP G12

In Moorish times, the Alfama was the grandest part of the city, but as Lisbon expanded, the new Christian nobility moved out, leaving it to the local fishing community. None of today's houses dates from before the Christian Recon-quest, but you'll notice a kasbah-like layout. Although an increasing number of fado restaurants are moving in, the quarter retains a quiet, village-like quality. Life continues much as it has done for years with people buying groceries and fish from hole-in-the-wall stores and householders stoking small outdoor charcoal grills. Half the fun of exploring here is getting lost, but head for Rua de São Miguel – off which run some of the most interesting *becos* (alleys) – and for the parallel street Rua de São Pedro.

SANTA ENGRÁCIA

Fado

Fado (literally "fate") is often described as a kind of Portuguese blues. Popular themes are love, death, bullfighting and indeed fate itself. It is believed to derive from music that was popular with eighteenth-century immigrants from Portugal's colonies who first settled in Alfama. Famous singers like Maria Severa and Amália Rodrigues grew up in Alfama, which since the 1930s has hosted some of the city's most authentic fado houses – stroll around after 8pm and you'll hear magical sounds emanating from various venues, or better still, enjoy a meal at one of the places listed on p.57. The big contemporary names are Ana Moura and Mariza, who grew up in neighbouring Mouraria. Other singers to look out for (though unlikely to appear in small venues) are Mizia, Carminho, Helder Moutinho, Carlos do Carmo, Maria da Fé and Cristina Branco.

IGREJA DE SANTO ESTÊVÃO

Largo de Santo Estêvão ☎ 213 912 600. Open for Sunday Mass only at 11am. Free. Tram #28. MAP PP.46–47. POCKET MAP G11

The handsome church of Santo Estêvão was built in 1733 and was partly damaged in the 1755 earthquake, leaving it with one of its two original towers. Its Baroque interior is impressive but is usually open only for Mass. However, its worth a visit if only to see the view over the river from it's terrace.

MUSEU DO FADO

Largo do Chafariz de Dentro 1 ☎ 218 823 470. ⓦ www.museudofado.pt. Tues–Sun 10am–6pm. €5. MAP PP.46–47, POCKET MAP G12

Set in the renovated Recinto da Praia, a former water cistern and bathhouse, the Museu do Fado provides an excellent introduction to this quintessentially Portuguese art form (see box above). It also has a good restaurant. The museum details the history of fado and its importance to the Portuguese people; its shop stocks a great selection of CDs. A series of rooms in the museum contains wax models, photographs, famous paintings of fado scenes and descriptions of the leading singers. It also traces the history of the Portuguese

guitar, an essential element of the fado performance. Interactive displays allow you to listen to the different types of fado (Lisbon has its own kind, differing from that of the northern city of Coimbra), varying from mournful to positively racy.

CRUISE TERMINAL

MAP PP.46–47, POCKET MAP H12

On most days, an overly large cruise-ship docks at the cruise terminal below the Alfama. The terminal is part of an ambitious riverfront redevelopment plan that has cleared away many of the old warehouses, to be replaced by an appealing pedestrianized walkway so that you can stroll along the Tagus all the way from Santa Apolónia train station to Praça do Comércio.

BARBADINHOS STEAM PUMPING STATION

Rua do Alviela 12 ☎ 218 100 215, ⓦ www .epal.pt. Tues–Sun 10am–12.30pm & 1.30–5.30pm. €5. POCKET MAP M5

Ten minutes' walk from Santa Apolónia metro, off Calçada dos Barbadinhos, the Barbadinhos Steam Pumping Station is a small but engaging museum housed in an attractive old pumping station filled with shiny brass, polished wood and Victorian ingenuity. It was built in 1880 to pump water from a nearby river up Lisbon's steep hills, depositing it in a reservoir hollowed out from a former Franciscan convent. It used four steam-powered engines that worked nonstop until 1928 and which you can see demonstrated today. The museum is the main branch of Lisbon's Museus da Água (water museums; see p.70 and p.102), and its exhibits give a fascinating insight into the evolution of the city's water supply.

MUSEU NACIONAL DO AZULEJO

Rua da Madre de Deus 4. Bus #794 from Praça do Comércio/Santa Apolónia ☏ 218 103 340, ⊕ www.mnazulejo.imc ip.pt. Tues–Sun 10am–6pm. €5, free 10am 2pm first Sunday every month. MAP PP.46–47, POCKET MAP M5

The Museu Nacional do Azulejo (tile museum) traces the development of Portuguese *azulejo* tiles from fifteenth-century Moorish styles to the present day, with each room representing a different period. Diverse styles range from seventeenth-century portraits of the English King Charles II with his Portuguese wife, Catherine of Bragança, to the 1720 satirical panel depicting a man being given an injection in his bottom. The museum is inside the church Madre de Deus, whose eighteenth-century tiled scenes of St Anthony are among the best in the city. Many of the rooms are housed round the church's cloisters – look for the spire in one corner of the main cloister, itself completely tiled. The highlight upstairs is Portugal's longest *azulejo* – a wonderfully detailed 40-metre panorama of Lisbon, completed in around 1738. The museum also has a good café-restaurant and shop.

Tram #28

The picture-book tram #28 (every 15min 5.40am–9.15pm; until 10.30pm on weekends) is one of the city's greatest rides, though its popularity is such that there are usually queues to get on and standing-room-only is more than likely. Built in England in the early twentieth century, the trams are all polished wood and chrome but give a distinctly rough ride up and down Lisbon's steepest streets, at times coming so close to shops that you could almost take a can of sardines off the shelves. From Graça, the tram plunges down through Alfama to the Baixa and up to Prazeres, to the west of the centre. Take care of belongings as pickpockets also enjoy the ride.

Shops

A ARTE DA TERRA

Rua de Augusto Rosa 40. Daily 11am–8pm.
MAP PP.46–47, POCKET MAP F12

Housed in the cathedral's historic stables – with some of the handicrafts displayed in the stone horse troughs – this is a beautiful space with a range of local arts and crafts, from jewellery and cork products to postcards, preserves and souvenirs.

CONSERVEIRA DE LISBOA

Rua dos Bacalhoeiras 34. Mon–Sat 9am–7pm. MAP PP.46–47, POCKET MAP E13

Wall-to-wall tin cans stuffed into wooden cabinets make this colourful 1930s shop a bizarre but intriguing place to stock up on tinned sardines, squid, salmon, mussels and just about any other sea beast you can think of.

SANTOS OFÍCIOS

Rua da Madalena 87. Mon–Sat 10am–8pm.
MAP PP.46–47, POCKET MAP E12

Small shop crammed with a somewhat touristy collection of regional crafts, but including some attractive ceramics, rugs, embroidery, baskets and toys.

CONSERVEIRA DE LISBOA

Restaurants

A MOURISCA

Largo da Graça 84–85. ☎ 218 863 688. Tues–Sun 9am–11pm. MAP PP.46–47, POCKET MAP F10

Bustling *cervejaria* whose draping of soccer scarves doesn't quite hide the beautifully tiled walls. There's a sizzling good range of fish and meat here, including pork steaks and squid kebabs (€10–11) and *arroz de marisco* (€25 for two people).

ARCO DO CASTELO

Rua do Chão da Feira 25 ☎ 218 876 598,
ⓦ www.arcodocastelo.wix.com. Mon–Sat noon–midnight. MAP PP.46–47, POCKET MAP F12

Cheerful place just below the entrance to the castle, specializing in moderately priced Goan dishes – there's a fine shrimp curry, and *feijoada indiana* (spicy bean stew). Mains are from €10.

BARRACÃO DE ALFAMA

Rua de S. Pedro 16 ☎ 218 866 359. Daily 11am–midnight. MAP PP.46–47, POCKET MAP G12

An unpretentious local *tasca* popular with locals, with non-touristy prices: you can have a full meal here for around €15. Portions are generous with fine fish and grills from under €10.

BICA DO SAPATO

Avda Infante Dom Henrique, Armazém B, Cais da Pedra à Bica do Sapato ☎ 218 810 320,
ⓦ www.bicadosapato.com. Mon 5pm–1am, Tues–Sat noon–1am. MAP PP.46–47, POCKET MAP M6

This stylish yet informal warehouse conversion has mirrored walls to reflect the crisp Tejo vistas. There's an outside terrace, too. The chef creates what he calls a "laboratory of Portuguese ingredients", including black pork with *migas* (garlic bread sauce) and tiger prawns as well as sushi. Satisfied guests have included Pedro Almodóvar, Catherine Deneuve and architect Frank Gehry, though its prices (mains €18–25) are about affordable to mere mortals.

CASANOVA

Avda Infante Dom Henrique, Loja 7 Armazém B, Cais da Pedra à Bica do Sapato ☎ 218 877 532, ⓦ www.pizzeriacasanova.pai.pt. Wed–Sun 12.30pm–2am. MAP PP.46–47, POCKET MAP M6

If *Bica do Sapato* is beyond your budget, the more modestly priced *Casanova* next door offers pizza, pasta and *crostini* accompanied by similar views from its terrace. It's very popular and you can't book, so turn up early. Expect to pay around €15 for a meal and drink.

ESTRELA DA SÉ

Largo S. António da Sé 4 ☎ 218 870 455. Mon–Sat noon–3pm & 7–10pm. MAP PP.46–47, POCKET MAP E12

Beautiful *azulejo*-covered restaurant near the Sé, serving inexpensive and tasty dishes like *alheira* (chicken sausage), salmon and Spanish-style tapas from €9. Its wooden booths – perfect for discreet trysts – date from the nineteenth century.

HUA TA LI

Rua dos Bacalhoeiros 109–115 ☎ 218 879 170, ⓦ www.restaurantechines.pt. Daily noon–3.30pm & 6.30–11pm. MAP PP.46–47, POCKET MAP E13

Great-value Chinese restaurant (mains from €7), very popular for Sunday lunch, when it heaves with diners (so it's best to book). Seafood scores highly; try the squid chop suey. It's also good for vegetarians.

MALMEQUER-BEMMEQUER

Rua de São Miguel 23–25 ☎ 218 876 535. Wed–Sun 12.30–3.30pm & 7–10pm, Tues 7–10pm; closed last week in Oct. MAP PP.46–47, POCKET MAP G12

Cheerily decorated and moderately priced place, overseen by a friendly owner. Grilled meat and fish dishes dominate the menu (try the *salmão no carvão* – charcoal-grilled salmon), or eat from the daily changing tourist menu – mains €11.

SANTA CLARA DOS COGUMELOS

Mercado de Santa Clara 7 ☎ 218 870 661, ⓦ www.santaclaradoscogumelos.com. Tues–Fri 7.30pm–11pm, Sat 12.30–3.30pm & 7.30–11pm. MAP PP.46–47, POCKET MAP H10

In a lovely room right above the market building, this Italian-run restaurant specializes in mushroom-themed dishes, and very tasty they are, too. Try mushroom risotto, gnocchi or salmon with mushroom sauce. Mains from €14.

SANTO ANTÓNIO DE ALFAMA

Beco de São Miguel 7 ☎ 218 881 328, ⓦ www.siteantonio.com. Daily 12.30pm–2am. MAP PP.46–47, POCKET MAP G12

With a lovely outdoor terrace shaded by vines and walls covered in black-and-white photos, this is one of the nicest restaurant-bars in the Alfama, with seating on three floors. There's a very long list of expensive wines; pasta and fish dishes from €13 or a range of less pricey tapas from €7.

VIA GRAÇA

Rua Damasceno Monteiro 9b ☎ 218 870 830, ⓦ www.restauranteviagraca.com. Mon–Fri 12.30–3pm & 7.30–11pm, Sat & Sun 7.30–11pm. MAP PP.46–47, POCKET MAP K5

Near the Miradouro da Graça, this sophisticated but highly rated restaurant in an unattractive modern building is better on the inside, from where you can soak up the stunning panoramas of Lisbon. Specialities include roast goat, game and *bacalhau* dishes from around €22–30.

Cafés

CRUZES CREDO

Rua Cruzes da Sé 29 ☎ 218 822 296. Daily 10.30am–2am. MAP PP.46–47, POCKET MAP F12

This fashionable little café has a jazzy ambience and serves tasty *petiscos* snacks including some unusual (for these parts) dishes such as bruschetta, hummus and burgers (€7–8). It's also a tranquil spot for a drink.

DELI DELUXE

Avda Infante Dom Henrique, Armazém B, Loja 8. Mon–Fri noon–midnight, Sat & Sun 10am–midnight (closes 10pm from Oct–Easter). MAP PP.46–47, POCKET MAP M6

A modern deli with delectable cheeses, cured meats and preserves, though the riverside café at the back is even more appealing. Grab a seat outdoors and enjoy the range of goodies from croissants to speciality teas, salads and cocktails.

POIS CAFÉ

Rua São João da Praça 93–95. Mon noon–11pm, Tues–Sun 10am–11pm. MAP PP.46–47, POCKET MAP F12

POIS CAFÉ

With its big comfy sofas and occasional art exhibitions, this high, arched-ceiling café is a must visit. There's a friendly, young crowd, books to dip into, cocktails, healthy brunches, light meals and home-made snacks, including a great *apfelstrudel*.

Bars and clubs

CHAPITÔ

Costa do Castelo 7 ☎ 218 867 734, ⊛ www .chapito.org. Restaurant Mon–Fri noon– midnight, Sat & Sun 7.30–midnight. Bar Mon–Fri 7pm–2am, Sat & Sun noon–2am. MAP PP.46–47, POCKET MAP E12

Multipurpose venue incorporating a theatre, circus school, restaurant and tapas bar. The restaurant, *Chapitô à Mesa*, is in an upstairs dining room, reached via a spiral staircase, and serves a range of menus with mains such as black pork with ginger and mushroom risotto from €16. The outdoor esplanade commands terrific views over Alfama and most people come here to drink and take in the view. Check the

DELI DELUXE

website for live music, films and readings.

LUX

Armazém A, Cais da Pedra a Santa Apolónia ⓦ www.luxfragil.com. Thurs–Sat 11pm–6.30am. MAP PP.46–47, POCKET MAP M6

This converted former meat warehouse has become one of Europe's most fashionable spaces, attracting A-list visitors such as Prince and Cameron Diaz. Part-owned by actor John Malkovich, it was the first place to venture into the docks opposite Santa Apolónia station. There's a rooftop terrace with amazing views, various bars, projection screens, a frenzied downstairs dancefloor, and music from pop and trance to jazz and dance. The club is also increasingly on the circuit for touring bands.

PORTAS DO SOL

Largo Portas do Sol ☎ 218 851 299, ⓦ www .portasdosol.biz. Daily 10am–2am. MAP PP.46–47, POCKET MAP G12

As you might guess from the name, this hip spot is an obligatory venue for anyone into sunsets. Hiding under the lip of the road, it's a chic indoor space, though most people head for the outside seats on the giant terrace with grandstand views over the Alfama. Pricey drinks, coffees and cocktails, but worth it. DJs on Fridays and Saturdays.

Fado and music venues

A BAIUCA

Rua de São Miguel 20 ☎ 218 867 284. Mon & Thurs–Sun 7.30–11pm. MAP PP.46–47, POCKET MAP G12

Nightly *fado vadio* ("casual" fado) is performed in this great little tiled *tasca* which serves decent fresh fish and grills; minimum spend is €25. Reservations advised.

A PARREIRINHA DE ALFAMA

Beco do Espírito Santo 1 ☎ 218 868 209, ⓦ www.parreirinhadaalfama.com. Tues–Sun 8pm–1am. MAP PP.46–47, POCKET MAP G12

One of the best fado venues owned by famous fado singer Argentina Santos, just off Largo do Chafariz de Dentro, often attracting leading stars and an enthusiastic local clientele. Reservations are advised when the big names appear.

CLUBE DE FADO

Rua de São João da Praça 86–94 ☎ 218 852 704, ⓦ www.clube-de-fado.com. Daily 8pm–2am. MAP PP.46–47, POCKET MAP F12

Intimate and homely fado club with stone pillars, an old well as a decorative feature, and a mainly local clientele. It attracts small-time performers, up-and-coming talent and the occasional big name. Expect to pay €60 or so including food.

CHAPITÔ

Chiado and Cais do Sodré

The well-to-do district of Chiado (pronounced she-ar-doo) is famed for its smart shops and cafés, along with the city's main museum for contemporary arts. Down on the waterfront, Cais do Sodré (pronounced kaiysh-doo-soodray) is one of the city's "in" districts. Many of its waterfront warehouses have been converted into upmarket cafés and restaurants and by day, in particular, a stroll along its characterful riverfront is very enjoyable. Nearby Mercado da Ribeira, Lisbon's main market, is also big on atmosphere, as is the hillside Bica district, which is served by another of the city's classic funicular street lifts – Elevador da Bica. Cais do Sodré is also where you can catch ferries across the Tejo to the little port of Cacilhas which not only has some great seafood restaurants with views over Lisbon, but is also the bus terminus for some of the region's best beaches and for the spectacular Cristo Rei statue of Christ.

RUA GARRETT

MAP P.59, POCKET MAP C12

Chiado's most famous street, Rua Garrett, is where you'll find some of the oldest shops and cafés in the city, including *A Brasileira* (see p.64). Beggars usually mark the nearby entrance to the **Igreja dos Mártires** (Church of the Martyrs), named after the English Crusaders who were killed during the siege of Lisbon. Some of the area's best shops can also be found in nearby Rua do Carmo. This was the heart of the area that was greatly damaged by a fire in 1988, although the original *belle époque* atmosphere has since been superbly re-created under the direction of eminent Portuguese architect Álvaro Siza Vieira.

RUA GARRETT

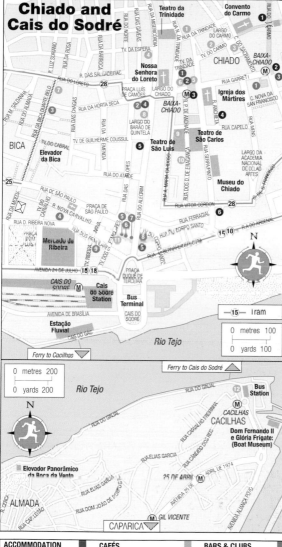

Chiado and Cais do Sodré

ACCOMMODATION		CAFÉS		BARS & CLUBS	
Hotel Bairro Alto	4	A Brasileira	6	A Tabacaria	9
Hotel Borges	2	Benard	5	Bar BA	2
Hotel do Chiado	3	Café Vertigo	2	Bicaense	3
Lisbon Poet's Hostel	1	Leitaria Académica	3	Café Tati	4
LX Boutique	5			Intermezzo	1
		RESTAURANTS		Music Box	8
SHOPS		Aqui há Peixe	1	Pensão Amor	7
A Vida Portuguesa	4	Cantinho do Avillez	10	Povo	5
Armazéns do Chiado	2	Casa Liège	7	Sol e Pesca	6
Fábrica Sant'Anna	5	Cervejaria Farol	12		
Livraria Bertrand	3	La Brasserie l'Entrecôte	8		
Luvaria Ulisses	1	Mini Bar	9		
Storytailors	6	Rio Grande	11		
		Tavares	4		

Tram #25 to Prazeres

You can catch another of Lisbon's classic tram rides, the #25, from the foot of the Elevador da Bica (Mon–Fri every 15min 6.30am–8.30pm). This sees far fewer tourists than tram #28 (see p.53) but takes almost as picturesque a route. From here it trundles along the riverfront and up through Lapa and Estrela to the suburb of Prazeres, best known as the site of one of Lisbon's largest cemeteries. You can stroll round the enormous plot where family tombs are movingly adorned with trinkets and photos of the deceased.

MUSEU DO CHIADO

Rua Serpa Pinto 4 ☎ 213 432 148, ⓦ www .museudochiado-ipmuseus.pt. Tues–Sun 10am–6pm. €4.50, free first Sun of the month. MAP P.59, POCKET MAP C13

The Museu do Chiado traces the history of art from Romanticism to Modernism. It is housed in a stylish building with a pleasant courtyard café and rooftop terrace, constructed around a nineteenth-century biscuit factory. Within the gallery's permanent collection are works by some of Portugal's most influential artists since the nineteenth century, along with foreign artists influenced by Portugal including Rodin. Highlights include Almada Negreiros' 1920s panels from the old São Carlos cinema, showing Felix the Cat; a beautiful sculpture, *A Viúva* (The Widow), by António Teixeira Lopes; and some evocative early twentieth-century Lisbon scenes by watercolourist Carlos Botelho. There are also frequent temporary exhibitions.

ELEVADOR DA BICA

Entrance on Rua de São Paulo. Mon–Sat 7am–9pm, Sun 9am–9pm. €3.60 return. MAP P.59, POCKET MAP B13

With its entrance tucked into an arch on Rua de São Paulo, the Elevador da Bica is one of the city's most atmospheric funicular railways. Built in 1892 – and originally powered by water counterweights, but now electrically operated – the *elevador* leads up towards the Bairro Alto, via a steep residential street. Take time to explore the steep side-streets of the Bica neighbourhood, too, a warren of characterful houses, little shops and fine local restaurants.

MERCADO DA RIBEIRA

Main entrance on Avda 24 de Julho ☎ 212 244 980. Fruit, fish and vegetable market Mon–Sat 6am–2pm; food stalls Sun–Wed 10am–midnight, Thurs–Sat 10am–2am. MAP P.59, POCKET MAP B13

The Mercado da Ribeira is Lisbon's most historic market. Built originally on the site of an old fort at the end of the nineteenth century, the current structure dates only from 1930. There's an impressive array of fresh fish, fruit and vegetables, with a separate, aromatic flower section. However, much of the building is now given over to a vibrant food hall, with an impressive range of stalls (most representing top chefs and well-known outlets in Lisbon) and plenty of benches to sit at. You pay slightly above the norm for the concept and ambience, but with everything from hams, cheeses and grilled chicken to gourmet burgers, seafood, organic salads and chocolates (not to mention champagne and cocktail bars), you might well find yourself tempted back here again and again. On Sundays there is a morning collectors' market.

RUA COR-DE-ROSA

POCKET MAP C13

Rua Nova do Carvalho's once dodgy clubs and bars have now (largely) been revamped into some of the city's coolest hangouts. The rebranding has extended to the colour of the street, which is now pink, hence the nickname Rua Cor-de-Rosa (Pink Street). We list some of the best places on p.65.

CACILHAS AND ALMADA

MAP P.59, POCKET MAP J8

The short, blustery ferry ride from Lisbon's Cais do Sodré over the Tejo to Cacilhas is great fun and grants wonderful views of the city. Cacilhas is little more than a bustling bus and ferry terminal with a pretty church, surrounded by lively stalls and cafés, but is well known for its seafood restaurants. You can also visit the wooden-hulled, fifty-gun **Dom Fernando II e Glória frigate** (☎917 841 149, ⓦwww.ccm.marinha.pt; Tues–Sun 10am–6pm (closes 5pm from Oct–April; €4) on Largo Alfredo Diniz. Built in India in 1843, it's now a museum showing what life at sea was like in the mid nineteenth century. A good riverside walk is to head west towards the bridge along the waterfront. It's around fifteen minutes' walk to the **Elevador Panorâmico da Boca do Vento** (daily 8am–midnight; €2 return), a sleek lift that whisks you 30m up the cliff face to the attractive old part of Almada, giving fantastic views.

C & STO REI

CRISTO REI

Bus #101 from outside the Cacilhas ferry terminal ☎212 751 000, ⓦwww.cristorei .pt. Lift open daily: June–Sept 9.30am–6.30pm; Oct–May 9.30am–6.15pm. €4 return. MAP P.59, POCKET MAP H9

On the heights above Almada stand the outstretched arms of *Cristo Rei* (Christ the King). Inspired by Rio's famous *Cristo Redentor* statue, it was built in 1959 as a pilgrimage site to grace Portugal's non-participation in World War II. A lift at the statue shuttles you a further 80m up to a dramatic viewing platform, from where, on a clear day, you can catch a glimpse of the glistening roof of the Pena palace at Sintra.

Travel to Cacilhas and beyond

Cais do Sodré is the main departure point for ferries over the Tejo to the largely industrial suburbs to the south. Ferries to Cacilhas (ⓦwww .transtejo.transporteslisboa.pt; every 15min, 5.20am–1.20am; €1.20 single) dock by a bus and tram depot from where buses run to Costa da Caparica (see p.129).

Shops

A VIDA PORTUGUESA

Rua Anchieta 11. Mon–Sat 10am–8pm, Sun 11am–8pm. MAP P.59, POCKET MAP C12

An expensive but evocative collection of retro toys, crafts and ceramics, beautifully displayed and packaged in a historic former perfumery.

ARMAZÉNS DO CHIADO

Rua do Carmo 2. Daily 10am–10pm, restaurants until 11pm. MAP P.59, POCKET MAP D12

This swish shopping centre sits on six floors above metro Baixa-Chiado in a structure that has risen from the ashes of the Chiado fire, though it retains its traditional facade. Various shops include branches of Pepe Jeans, FNAC, Bodyshop and Sunglass Hut. The top floor has a series of cafés and restaurants, including Brazilian chain *Chimarrão*, most offering great views.

FÁBRICA SANT'ANNA

Rua do Alecrim 95. Mon–Sat 9.30am–7pm. MAP P.59, POCKET MAP C13

If you're interested in Portuguese *azulejos*, check out this factory shop, founded in 1741, which sells copies of traditional designs and a great range of handmade ceramics.

LIVRARIA BERTRAND

Rua Garrett 73. Mon–Sat 9am–10pm, Sun 11am–8pm. MAP P.59, POCKET MAP C12

Officially the world's oldest bookshop, founded in 1773 and once the meeting place for Lisbon's literary set. Offering novels in English and a range of foreign magazines, it's also a good place to find English translations of Portuguese writers including Fernando Pessoa.

LUVARIA ULISSES

Rua do Carmo 87a. Mon–Sat 10am–7pm. MAP P.59, POCKET MAP D11

STORYTAILORS

The superb, ornately carved wooden doorway leads you into a minuscule glove shop, with hand-wear to suit all tastes tucked into rows of boxes.

STORYTAILORS

Calçada do Ferragial 8. Tues–Sat 11am–9pm. MAP P.59, POCKET MAP C13

Set in a suitably stylish, bare-brick eighteenth-century former warehouse, the shop interior is as magical as its designer clothes inspired by fairy tales. Its haute couture range has been snapped up by the likes of Madonna and Lily Allen, though you'll need a rock star's salary to afford it.

Restaurants

AQUI HÁ PEIXE

Rua da Trindade 18a ☎ 213 432 154, ⓦ www.aquihapeixe.pt. Tues–Sun 11am–2am. MAP P.59, POCKET MAP C12

Meaning "We've got fish here", this stylish, if pricey, seafood restaurant has been making waves even with Lisboetas who know a thing or two about the sea's produce. Classic fish dishes are served with panache – sublime tuna steaks, prawns cooked in garlic, clams cooked with coriander, plus a few meat dishes, all from around €18, in a neat fish-themed interior.

CANTINHO DO AVILLEZ

Rua dos Duques de Bragança 7 ☎ 211 992 369, ⓦ www.cantinhodoavillez.pt. Mon–Sat 12.30–3pm & 7pm–midnight. MAP P.59, POCKET MAP C13

In a contemporary space, with tram #28 rattling by its door, this laidback but classy canteen is the place to sample food from Lisbon's top chef, José Avillez. Delectable mains from €17–21 include the likes of scallops with sweet potatoes and asparagus or Alentejo pork with coriander. Starters include a superb baked Nisa cheese and the house wines are equally top-notch.

CASA LIÈGE

Rua da Bica Duarte Belo 72–74 ☎ 213 422 774. Mon–Sat 11am–11pm. MAP P.59, POCKET MAP B12

Small and bustling *tasca* at the top end of the Elevador da Bica, packed at lunchtimes thanks to filling and inexpensive dishes such as grilled chicken, sausages and fine *pastéis de bacalhau* from under €8. Good house wine, too.

CERVEJARIA FAROL

Alfredo Dinis Alex 1–3, Cacilhas ☎ 212 765 248, ⓦ www.restaurantefarol.com. Daily 10am–midnight. MAP P.59, POCKET MAP H9

The most high-profile seafood restaurant in Cacilhas, with fine views across the Tejo to match. If you feel extravagant, it's hard to beat the lobsters, though other fish dishes are yours from around €12. *Azulejos* on the wall show the old *farol* (lighthouse) that once stood here – the restaurant is located along the quayside, on the right as you leave the ferry.

LA BRASSERIE L'ENTRECÔTE

Rua do Alecrim 117–120 ☎ 213 473 616, ⓦ www.brasserieentrecote.pt. Daily 12.30–3pm & 7.30–11.30pm. MAP P.59, POCKET MAP C12

This upmarket restaurant has won awards for its entrecôte steak which is just as well, as that's all it serves. With a sauce said to contain 35 ingredients, it is truly delicious. Mains from €18–25. Reservations advised.

MINI BAR

Rua António Maria Cardoso 58 ☎ 211 305 393, ⓦ www.minibar.pt. Daily 7pm–1am. MAP P.59, POCKET MAP C12

There's certainly a theatrical element to the cuisine in this buzzy restaurant-bar inside the Art Deco Teatro de São Luis. Various themed tasting menus feature innovative and quirky tapas-style dishes (€3–13) including Algarve prawns, tuna and mackerel cerviche and beef croquettes. Some of top chef José Avillez's creations are decidedly Blumenthalesque, including amazing 'edible' cocktails and 'exploding' olives. Highly recommended.

RIO GRANDE

Rua Nova do Carvalho 55 ☎ 213 423 804. Mon, Tues & Thurs–Sun 12.30pm–3pm & 6–11pm. MAP P.59, POCKET MAP B12

It might be on a street full of hip bars, but Rio Grande is reassuringly traditional, with *azulejos* on the walls beneath an arched ceiling. The spacious restaurant serves up good-value Portuguese classics such as pork steaks and a good array of fresh fish for under €9.

CERVEJARIA FAROL

TAVARES

TAVARES

Rua da Misericórdia 37 ☎ 213 421 112, ⓦ www.restaurantetavares.net. Tues–Sat 7.30–11pm. MAP P.59, POCKET MAP C12

Lisbon's oldest restaurant, dating from 1784, is a riot of gilt and mirrors, a fitting setting to try the best of modern Portuguese cuisine. Crab and clam *açorda*, partridge, scabbard fish with yoghurt and *bacalhau* often feature in the €60 menu of four dishes. Mains around €30, or a five-course tasting menu from €70.

Cafés

A BRASILEIRA

Rua Garrett 120. Daily 8am–2am. MAP P.59, POCKET MAP C12

Opened in 1905, and marked by an outdoor bronze statue of the poet Fernando Pessoa, this is the most famous of Lisbon's old-style coffee houses. The tables on the pedestrianized street get snapped up by tourists but the real appeal is in its traditional interior, where prices are considerably cheaper, especially if you stand at the long bar. At night buskers often

add a frisson as the clientele changes to a more youthful brigade, all on the beer.

BENARD

Rua Garrett 104. Mon–Sat 8am–midnight. MAP P.59, POCKET MAP C12

Often overlooked because of its proximity to *A Brasileira*, this ornate nineteenth-century café offers superb cakes, ice cream and coffees; it also has a hugely popular outdoor terrace on Chiado's most fashionable street.

CAFÉ VERTIGO

Trav do Carmo 4 ☎ 213 433 112. Mon–Thurs 11am–7pm, Fri & Sat 11am–midnight. MAP P.59, POCKET MAP C12

An arty crowd frequents this bare-brick-walled café with an ornate glass ceiling. Occasional art exhibits and a good range of cakes and organic snacks.

LEITARIA ACADÉMICA

Largo do Carmo 1–3. Mon–Sat 7am–11pm, Sun 7am–8pm. MAP P.59, POCKET MAP C12

Outdoor tables on one of the city's leafiest squares. Besides drinks and snacks, it also does light lunches; the tasty grilled sardines are perfect in summer.

Bars and clubs

A TABACARIA

Rua de São Paulo 75–77 ☎ 213 420 281. Mon–Fri noon–1am, Sat 6pm–2am. MAP P.59, POCKET MAP B13

In a wonderful old tobacco shop dating back to 1885 – with many of the original fittings – this cosy bar specializes in cocktails (from €7), made from gin, vodka, whisky and seasonal fruits.

BAR BA

Praça Luís de Camões 8. Daily 11pm–1.30pm. MAP P.59, POCKET MAP C12

Swish and stylish split-level hotel bar, with a giant triangular table in the main area, a downstairs video-room and laidback lounge area. Pricey drinks come with generous bowls of nuts. DJs man the decks from 8pm most nights of the week.

BICAENSE

Rua da Bica Duarte Belo 38–42. Tues–Sat 8pm–2am. MAP P.59, POCKET MAP B12

Small, fashionable bar on the steep street used by the Elevador da Bica, with occasional live jazz and Latin sounds; good cocktails and a moderately priced bar-food menu.

CAFÉ TATI

Rua da Ribeira Nova 36 ⓣ 213 461 279, ⓦ www.cafetati.blogspot.com. Tues–Sun 11am–1am. MAP P.59, POCKET MAP B13

One of the new breed of arty café-bars opening in the area around the market. With stripped walls and old furniture, this has tatty-chic decor and an array of snacks, teas, cakes and wines. Popular for Sunday brunch, it is also lively on Wednesday and Sunday evenings when there's live jazz.

INTERMEZZO

Rua Garrett Patio 19. Mon–Sat 12.30pm–11pm. MAP P.59, POCKET MAP D12

With outside seats in a hidden courtyard, this stylish little modern bar does a mean range of cocktails and other drinks; its sister *Mezo Giorno* next door also serves decent pizzas.

MUSIC BOX

Rua Nova do Carvalho 24 ⓣ 213 430 107, ⓦ www.musicboxlisboa.com. Mon–Sat 11pm–6am. MAP P.59, POCKET MAP C13

Tucked under the arches of Rua Nova do Carvalho is this cool cultural and music venue which hosts club nights, live music, films and performing arts, with an emphasis on promoting independent acts. There's a top sound and light system and usually a buzzy, happy crowd.

PENSÃO AMOR

Rua do Alecrim 19 ⓣ 213 143 399. Mon–Wed & Sun noon–2am, Thurs–Sat noon–4am. MAP P.59, POCKET MAP C13

The "Pension of Love" is a former "house of ill-repute". It has retained its eighteenth-century burlesque fittings for its current incarnation as a trendy bar with risqué photos, frescoes and mirrors. You can browse through the small erotic bookstore or enjoy occasional live concerts.

POVO

Rua Nova do Carvalho 32–26 ⓣ 213 473 403. Daily 6pm–4am. MAP P.59, POCKET MAP C13

This fashionable tavern offers fado from up-and-coming stars (Tues–Thurs and Sun from 9.30pm) and late-night DJs at weekends in the heart of "Pink Street". There's a great menu of *petiscos* and mains such as mussels with seaweed, *bacalhau* dishes and steaks (€8–21).

SOL E PESCA

Rua Nova do Carvalho 44 ⓣ 213 467 203. Daily noon–2am. MAP P.59, POCKET MAP C13

Once a shop selling fishing equipment, this is now a hip bar. The fishing equipment is now part of the decor, and you can still purchase tinned fish to enjoy with bread and wine at low stools inside, or outside on trendy "Pink Street".

PESSOA STATUE, A BRASILEIRA

Bairro Alto and São Bento

The Bairro Alto, the Upper Town, sits on a hill west of the Baixa. After the 1755 earthquake, the relatively unscathed district became the favoured haunt of Lisbon's young bohemians. Home to the Institute of Art and Design and various designer boutiques, it is still the city's most fashionable district. By day, the central grid of narrow, cobbled streets feels residential. After dark, however, the area throngs with people visiting its famed fado houses, bars and restaurants, while the city's gay community coalesces around the clubs of neighbouring Príncipe Real. There are impressive monuments too, including the Palácio da Assembléia, Portugal's parliamentary building in nearby São Bento. This area houses good ethnic restaurants, a legacy of the city's first black community established by the descendants of African slaves.

ELEVADOR DA GLÓRIA

Mon–Thurs 7am–11.55pm, Fri 7am–12.25am, Sat 8.30am–12.25am, Sun 9am–11.55pm. €3.60 return. MAP PP.68–69, POCKET MAP C11

Everyone should ride the Elevador da Glória at least once. From the bottom of Calçada da Glória (off Praça dos Restauradores, see p.38), the funicular climbs the knee-jarringly sheer street in a couple of minutes, leaving the lower city behind as you ascend above its rooftops. An amazing feat of engineering, the tram system was built in 1885. It was originally powered by water displacement, later replaced by steam, and now runs on electricity.

At the top, pause at the gardens, the **Miradouro de São Pedro de Alcântara**, from where there's a superb view across the city to the castle.

ELEVADOR DA GLÓRIA

IGREJA DE SÃO ROQUE

Largo de Trindade Coelha ☎ 213 235 383.
ⓦ www.museu-saoroque.com. Mon 2–7pm,
April–Sept Tues–Sun 9am–7pm, Oct–March
Tues–Sun 9am–6pm. Free. MAP PP.68–69,
POCKET MAP C11

The sixteenth-century Igreja de
São Roque looks like the plainest
church in the city, with its bleak
Renaissance facade. Yet inside
lies an astonishing succession of
lavishly decorated side chapels.
The highlight is the **Capela de
São João Baptista**, for its size
the most expensive chapel ever
constructed. It was ordered from
Rome in 1742 by Dom João V to
honour his patron saint and,
more dubiously, to gratify Pope
Benedict XIV whom he had
persuaded to confer a
patriarchate on Lisbon. It was
erected at the Vatican for the
Pope to celebrate Mass in, before
being dismantled and shipped to
Lisbon at the then vast cost of
£250,000. If you examine the
four "oil paintings" of John the
Baptist's life, you'll find that they
are in fact intricately worked
mosaics. The more valuable
parts of the altar front are kept
in the adjacent **museum** (same
hours as church; €2.50, free Sun
9am–2pm), which also displays
sixteenth- to eighteenth-century
paintings and a motley
collection of church relics.

CONVENTO DO CARMO

Largo do Carmo ☎ 213 478 629, ⓦ www
.museuarqueologicodocarmo.pt. Mon–Sat:
June–Sept 10am–7pm; Oct–May 10am–6pm.
€3.50. MAP P.59, POCKET MAP D12

Built between 1389 and 1423,
and once the largest church in
the city, the Convento do Carmo
was partially destroyed by the
1755 earthquake but is even
more striking as a result with its
beautiful Gothic arches rising
grandly into the sky. Today it
houses the splendid **Museu
Arqueológico do Carmo**, home

CONVENTO DO CARMO

to many of the treasures from
monasteries that were dissolved
after the 1834 revolution. The
entire nave is open to the
elements, with columns and
statuary scattered in all corners.
Inside, on either side of what
was the main altar, are the main
exhibits, centring on a series of
tombs. Largest is the beautifully
carved, stone tomb of Ferdinand
I; nearby, that of Gonçalo de
Sousa, chancellor to Henry
the Navigator, is topped by a
statue of Gonçalo himself. There
is also an Egyptian sarcophagus,
whose inhabitant's feet are just
visible underneath the lid; and,
equally alarmingly, two
pre-Columbian mummies which
lie in glass cases, alongside the
preserved heads of a couple of
Peruvian Indians.

The exit to the **Elevador de
Santa Justa** (see p.37) is at the
side of the Convento do Carmo
– go onto the rampway leading
to it for fine views over the city
or the partly-lawned terrace in
front, the **Terraços do Carmo**,
with its handy café.

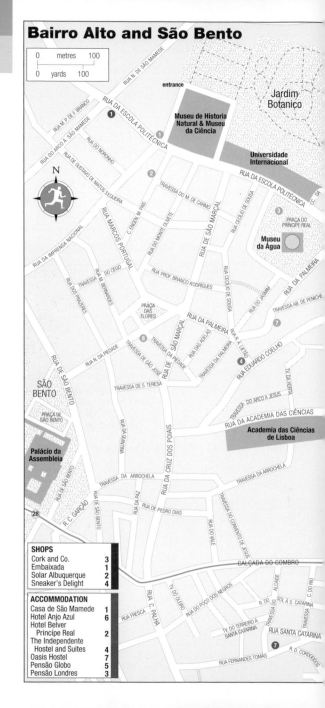

Bairro Alto and São Bento

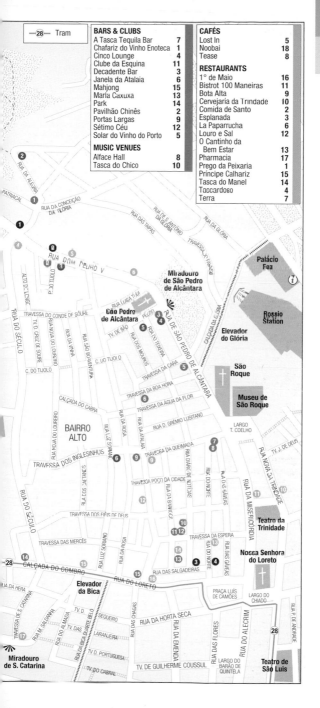

—28— Tram

BARS & CLUBS

A Tasca Tequila Bar	7
Chafariz do Vinho Enoteca	1
Cinco Lounge	4
Clube da Esquina	11
Decadente Bar	3
Janela da Atalaia	6
Mahjong	15
Marla Caxuxa	13
Park	14
Pavilhão Chinês	2
Portas Largas	9
Sétimo Céu	12
Solar do Vinho do Porto	5

MUSIC VENUES

Alface Hall	8
Tasca do Chico	10

CAFÉS

Lost In	5
Noobai	18
Tease	8

RESTAURANTS

1º de Maio	16
Bistrot 100 Maneiras	11
Bota Alta	9
Cervejaria da Trindade	10
Comida de Santo	2
Esplanada	3
La Paparrucha	6
Louro e Sal	12
O Cantinho da Bem Estar	13
Pharmacia	17
Prego da Peixaria	1
Príncipe Calhariz	15
Tasca do Manel	14
Toccardoso	4
Terra	7

BAIRRO ALTO NIGHTLIFE

BAIRRO ALTO

MAP PP.68-69, POCKET MAP B11

Quiet by day, the graffitied central streets of the Bairro Alto buzz with people after dark, especially on summer weekends when the streets become a giant mass of partygoers. The most lively area is the tight network of streets to the west of Rua da Misericórdia, particularly after midnight in Rua do Norte, Rua Diário de Notícias, Rua da Atalaia and Rua da Rosa. Running steeply downhill, Rua do Século is one of the area's most historic streets. A sign at no. 89 marks the birthplace of the Marquês de Pombal, the minister responsible for rebuilding Lisbon after the Great Earthquake.

MIRADOURO DE SANTA CATARINA

Tram #28. MAP P.59, POCKET MAP A12

At the bottom end of the Bairro Alto grid, set on the cusp of a hill high above the river, the railed Miradouro de Santa Catarina has spectacular views. Here, in the shadow of the statue of the Adamastor – a mythical beast from Luís de Camões's *Lusiads* – a mixture of oddballs and New Age types often collects around an alluring drinks kiosk (daily

10am–dusk, weather permitting), which has a few outdoor tables.

PRAÇA DO PRÍNCIPE REAL

Bus #758 from Chiado. MAP PP.68-69, POCKET MAP A10

North of the Bairro Alto, the streets open out around the leafy Praça do Príncipe Real, one of the city's loveliest squares. Laid out in 1860 and surrounded by the ornate homes of former aristocrats – now mostly shops or offices – the square is the focal point of Lisbon's gay scene, though by day it is largely populated by families or locals playing cards under the trees.

MUSEU DA ÁGUA PRÍNCIPE REAL

Praça do Príncipe Real 1. Bus #758 from Chiado ☎ 218 100 215, ⬿ www.epal.pt. Tues–Sat 10am–5.30pm. €2. Tours Wed & Sat 11am & 3pm, €2. MAP PP.68-69, POCKET MAP A10

The Museu da Água Príncipe Real is accessed down steps in the centre of the square of the same name. Inside is an eerie nineteenth-century reservoir, where you can admire brick and vaulted ceilings, part of a network of tunnels that link up with the Aqueduto das Águas Livres (see p.102). Tours – not for claustrophobics – take you along one of these, a humid 410m tunnel that exits at the viewpoint of Miradouro de São Pedro (see p.66).

MUSEUS NACIONAL DE HISTÓRIA E DA CIÊNCIA

Rua Escola Politécnica 56. Bus #758 from Chiado ⬿ www.museus.ulisboa.pt. Tues–Fri 10am–5pm, Sat & Sun 11am–6pm; closed Aug. €5, combined ticket €6, includes entry to Jardim Botânico, free Thurs 5–8pm. MAP PP.68-69, POCKET MAP H5

The nineteenth-century Neoclassical former technical college now hosts the mildly engaging museums of natural history known as the Museus de

Politécnica. The **Museu da Ciência** (whose labs featured in the film *The Promise*, starring Christian Bale) has some absorbing geological exhibits and a low-tech interactive section where you can balance balls on jets of air and swing pendulums among throngs of school kids.

The **Museu da História Natural** houses a rather dreary collection of stuffed animals, eggs and shells, though temporary exhibitions can be more diverting.

JARDIM BOTÂNICO

Rua Escola Politécnica 58 ☏ 213 971 800, ⓦ www.museus.ulisboa.pt. Daily: April–Oct 9am–8pm; Nov–March 9am–6pm. €2 gardens or €6 for combined ticket to Museus de História e da Ciência. MAP PP.68–69, POCKET MAP H5

The lush botanical gardens are almost invisible from the surrounding streets and provide a tranquil escape from the city bustle. The Portuguese explorers introduced many plant species to Europe during the golden age of exploration and these gardens, laid out between 1858 and 1878, are packed with twenty thousand neatly labelled species from around the world. Shady paths lead downhill under towering palms and luxuriant shrubs past a "Lugar tagio" greenhouse for breeding butterflies.

PALÁCIO DA ASSEMBLÉIA

Rua de São Bento. Tram #28. MAP PP.68–69, POCKET MAP H6

Below the Bairro Alto in the district of São Bento, you can't miss the late sixteenth-century Neoclassical facade of the Palácio da Assembléia. Formerly a Benedictine monastery, it was taken over by the government in 1834 and today houses the Assembléia da República, Portugal's **parliament**; it's not open to the public, though you can book a tour by special arrangement (☏ 213 919 625, ⓦ www.parlamento.pt). Most visitors make do with the view of its steep white steps from tram #28 as it rattles along Calçada da Estrela, though it is worth exploring the earthy streets nearby. This was where Lisbon's black community put down roots – Rua do Poço dos Negros (Black Man's Well) takes its awful name from the corpses of slaves tossed into a hole here.

CASA MUSEU AMÁLIA RODRIGUES

Rua de São Bento 193 ☏ 213 971 896, ⓦ www.amaliarodrigues.pt. Tues–Sun 10am–1pm & 2–6pm. €5. Bus #706 from Cais do Sodré, or a short walk from tram #28. MAP PP.68–69, POCKET MAP G6

The daughter of an Alfama orange-seller, Amália Rodrigues was the undisputed queen of fado music until her death in 1999. The house where she lived since the 1950s has been kept as it was, and you can also admire original posters advertising her performances on stage and in the cinema, portraits by Portuguese artists and some of her personal possessions.

JARDIM BOTÂNICO

Shops

CORK AND CO.

Rua das Salgadeiras 10 Ⓦ www.corkand
company.pt. Mon–Thurs 11am–7pm,
Fri & Sat 11am–9pm. MAP PP.68–69,
POCKET MAP B12

Portugal supplies around fifty
percent of the world's cork,
and this stylish shop displays
the versatility of the product
with a range of tasteful cork
goods, from bags and
bracelets to umbrellas.

EMBAIXADA

Praça do Príncipe Real 26 Ⓣ 963 309 154,
Ⓦ www.embaixadalx.pt. Daily noon–8pm.
MAP PP.68–69, POCKET MAP A10

Housed in a former pseudo-
Moorish palace overlooking
Praça do Príncipe Real, this
is a beautiful upmarket
emporium where boutiques
showcase Portugal's leading
names in fashion. There are
designer clothes, shoes and
crafts along with temporary
exhibits and a café-bar-
restaurant in a wonderfully
ornate room.

SNEAKER'S DELIGHT

Rua do Norte 30–32. Mon–Sat 1–10pm. MAP
PP.68–69, POCKET MAP C12

A typical example of Bairro
Alto creativity – limited
edition sneakers and a few
designer clothes in a sparse
space dotted with bits of
old TVs and computers that
are a work of art in their
own right.

SOLAR ALBUQUERQUE

Rua Dom Pedro V 70. Mon–Fri 10am–7pm,
Sat 10am–1pm. Closed Sat in July and Aug.
MAP PP.68–69, POCKET MAP B10

A huge treasure-trove of
antique tiles, plates and
ceramics dating back to the
sixteenth century – great for
a browse.

SOLAR ALBUQUERQUE

Restaurants

1° DE MAIO

Rua da Atalaia 8 Ⓣ 213 426 840. Mon–Fri
noon–3pm & 7–10.30pm, Sat noon–3pm.
MAP PP.68–69, POCKET MAP B12

Naked Chef-style food: simple
slabs of grilled fish and meat
with boiled veg and chips.
You can watch the cook
through a hatch at the back,
adding to the theatrics of a
bustling, traditional *adega*
(wine cellar) with a low,
arched ceiling. Mains are
around €10–12. Get there
early to be sure of a table.

BISTROT 100 MANEIRAS

Largo da Trindade 9 Ⓣ 210 990 575. Mon–Sat
7.30pm–2am. MAP PP.68–69, POCKET MAP C11

In a fine Art Nouveau building
with film-inspired decor,
Sarajevo-born chef Ljubmar
Stanisic produces a fascinating
mixture of classy mains (sea
urchin with scrambled egg,
game pie and roast goat,
around €25) and comfort foods
such as salmon burgers and
risotto (€18).

BOTA ALTA

Trav da Queimada 37 ☎ 213 427 959. Mon–
Fri noon–2.30pm & 7–10.30pm, Sat 7–10pm.
MAP PP.68–69, POCKET MAP B11

Tavern decorated with old
boots (*botas*) and an eclectic
picture collection. It attracts
queues for its vast portions of
sensibly priced, traditional
Portuguese food – including
bacalhau com natas (cod
cooked in cream) and fine
cakes. The tables are crammed
in and it's always packed; try to
arrive before 8pm or book in
advance. Mains from €11.

CERVEJARIA DA TRINDADE

Rua Nova da Trindade 20 ☎ 213 423 506
Sun–Thurs 10am–midnight, Fri & Sat
10am–1am MAP PP.68–69, POCKET MAP C11

The city's oldest beer-hall dates
from 1836. At busy times you'll
be shown to your table; at
others find a space in the
original vaulted hall, decorated
with *azulejos*, depicting the
elements and seasons. Shellfish
is the speciality, though other
fish and meat dishes (from €12)
are lighter on the wallet. There
is also a patio garden and – a
rarity – a children's menu.

COMIDA DE SANTO

Calçada Engenheiro Miguel Pais 39
☎ 213 963 339. Mon & Wed–Sun
12.30–3.30pm & 7.30pm–1am; evenings only
in Aug. MAP PP.68–69, POCKET MAP H6

Late-opening, slightly pricey
Brazilian restaurant serving
cocktails and classic dishes such
as *feijoada a brasileira* (Brazilian
bean stew) and a fantastic
ensopadinho de peixe (fish in
coconut), with good vegetarian
options. Mains around €18–20.

ESPLANADA

Praça do Príncipe Real ☎ 962 311 669. Daily
9am–11pm. MAP PP.68–69, POCKET MAP A10

A good range of quiches and
chunky sandwiches makes this
an ideal and inexpensive lunch
spot. The outdoor tables set
under the trees get snapped up
quickly, though the glass
pavilion comes into its own
when the weather turns. It's
also a popular gay haunt.

LA PAPARRUCHA

Rua Dom Pedro V 18–20 ☎ 213 425 333.
Mon–Fri noon–3pm & 6–11.30pm, Sat & Sun
12.30–3.30pm & 6–11.30pm. MAP PP.68–69,
POCKET MAP B10

The best feature of this
Argentinian restaurant is the
fantastic back room and terrace
offering superb views over the
Baixa. The food is recom-
mended too, with steaks, fish
and pasta options. Mains from
€14, with good-value lunchtime
buffets from around €13.

LOURO E SAL

Rua da Atalaia 55 ☎ 213 476 275. Daily except
Tues 7pm–1am. MAP PP.68–69, POCKET MAP B12

Typical of a new breed of
fashionable restaurants in the
area, offering good-value,
nouveau Portuguese cuisine
such as beef with coffee and
mushroom sauce, with mains
from around €10.

BOTA ALTA

O CANTINHO DO BEM ESTAR

Rua do Norte 46 ☎ 213 464 265. Tues–Sun
noon–2.30pm & 7.15–11.30pm. MAP PP.68–69.
POCKET MAP C12

Small and popular, the
"canteen of well-being" lives
up to its name: get there
early to guarantee a place.
From the menu, the rice
dishes and generous salads are
the best bet.

PHARMACIA

Rua Marechal Saldanha 1 ☎ 213 462 146.
Tues–Sun 1pm–1am. MAP PP.68–69. POCKET MAP A12

Part of the Pharmaceutical
Society and Museum, this
traditional building on lawns
facing the Tejo is a terrific spot
for a quirky café-restaurant
decked out with retro
pharmacy fittings. The
speciality here is tapas (from
around €7). Enjoy daily specials
in the evening, or just pop in
for a drink.

PREGO DA PEIXARIA

Rua Escola Politécnica 40 ☎ 213 471 356.
Daily 12.30pm–1am. MAP PP.68–69, POCKET MAP H5

Traditional *pregos* are steak
sandwiches, but this
fashionable restaurant has
embraced a whole host of
varieties. Choose from the likes
of *bacalhau*, tuna, mushroom
or salmon with octopus; all are
delicious and around €9–13.
There's a cool interior

courtyard and fittings made
from recycled materials.

PRÍNCIPE CALHARIZ

Calçado do Combro 28–30 ☎ 213 420 971.
Mon–Fri & Sun noon–3pm & 7–10.30pm.
MAP PP.68–69, POCKET MAP B12

Here's a place that's reliable,
good value, has plenty of tables,
generous portions – and a local
buzz. Recommended are the
porco Portuguesa (fried pork
cubes with fried potatoes) and
the salmon steaks. Leave room
for the rich chocolate mousse.
Mains from €9.

TASCA DO MANEL

Rua da Barroca 24 ☎ 213 463 813. Daily
noon–3pm & 6.30–11pm. MAP PP.68–69.
POCKET MAP B12

One of the dying breed of
inexpensive *tascas*, still
attracting a largely local crowd
for wholesome dishes such as
wild boar, grilled salmon or
bean stew from around €10–12
with outdoor seats in summer.

TASCARDOSO

Rua Dom Pedro V 137 ☎ 213 427 578.
Mon–Sat noon–3pm & 7pm–midnight.
MAP PP.68–69, POCKET MAP A10

Go through the stand-up bar
and down the stairs to the tiny
eating area for excellent and
inexpensive tapas-style meats
and cheeses and good-value
hot dishes from around €7–12.

TERRA

Rua da Palmeira 15 ☎ 213 421 407.
Tues–Sun 12.30–3.30pm & 7.30–10pm.
MAP PP.68–69, POCKET MAP A10

Attractive vegetarian and
vegan restaurant with a lovely
patio garden serving veggie
versions of classic Portuguese
dishes. The all-you-can-eat
buffets are good value at
around €16; leave room for
the Italian ice creams.

Cafés

LOST IN

Rua Dom Pedro V 56 ☎ 917 759 282. Mon
4pm–midnight, Tues–Sun 12.30pm midnight.
MAP PP.68–69, POCKET MAP B10

This Indian-inspired little
café-restaurant has a great
terrace with exhilarating views
over town. The menu features
prawn curry and veggie
burgers (€12–14), or just pop
in for a drink.

NOOBAI

Miradouro do Adamastor, Rua de Catarina
☎ 213 465 014, Ⓦ www.noobaicafe.com.
Tues–Thurs noon–10pm, Fri & Sat
noon–midnight, Sun noon–8pm. MAP PP.68–69,
POCKET MAP A12

Modern, jazzy café-restaurant
with a superb terrace just below
Miradouro de Santa Catarina.
Fabulous views complement
the inexpensive fresh juices,
tapas, quiches and the like.

TEASE

Rua Nova da Piedade 15 ☎ 914 447 383,
Ⓦ www.tease.pt. Mon–Thurs 9am–9pm,
Fri–Sat 9am–11pm. MAP PP.68–69, POCKET MAP H6

Specializing in amazing
cupcakes and chocolate
goodies, this hip, tiled café with
jazzy sounds also teases your
tastebuds with juices,
smoothies and inexpensive
light lunches such as quiches
and salads.

Bars and clubs

A TASCA TEQUILA BAR

Trav da Queimada 13–15 ☎ 915 617 805.
Daily 6pm–3am. MAP PP.68–69, POCKET MAP C11

Colourful Mexican bar with
Latin sounds, which caters to
a good-time crowd downing
tequilas, margaritas and
Brazilian *caipirinhas*.

CHAFARIZ DO VINHO ENOTECA

Rua da Mae de Água ☎ 213 422 079. Tues–
Sun 6pm–2am. MAP PP.68–69, POCKET MAP A10

This extraordinary wine bar
is set in the bowels of a
nineteenth-century bathhouse
whose underground tunnels
once piped water into Lisbon.
The bar offers a long list of
Portuguese wines, which
you can enjoy with regional
breads and assorted *petiscos*
(snacks) such as oysters or
dates with bacon. It gets busy at
weekends so it's best to reserve
if you want to eat, though you
can always squeeze in for a
drink or sit at one of the
outside tables.

CHAFARIZ DO VINHO ENOTECA

CINCO LOUNGE

Rua Ruben A. Leitão 17a Ⓦwww.cincolounge
.com. Daily 9pm–2am. MAP PP.68–69, POCKET MAP A11

A New York-style cocktail
lounge run by Brits in the heart
of Lisbon – there are over a
hundred cocktails to choose
from; go for one of the wacky
fruit concoctions (anyone for
gin, lime and dandelion?) while
sinking into one of the
enormous comfy sofas.

CLUBE DA ESQUINA

Rua da Barroca 30 ☎ 929 092 742. Mon–Thurs
7pm–2am, Fri & Sat 7pm–3am. MAP PP.68–69,
POCKET MAP B12

Buzzing little corner bar with
ancient radios on the walls and
DJs spinning discs. Attracts a
young crowd enjoying vast
measures of spirits.

DECADENTE BAR

Rua de São Pedro de Alcântara 81 ☎ 213 461
281, Ⓦ www.thedecadente.pt. Sun–Wed
noon–11pm, Thurs noon–1am, Fri & Sat
noon–2am. MAP PP.68–69, POCKET MAP B10

Attached to a boutique hostel,
this small, fashionable bar and
restaurant attracts a youthful,
laidback crowd. It's best on
Thursday and Saturday evening
when there is often live music,
usually Latin or jazz.

JANELA DA ATALAIA

Rua da Atalaia 160 ☎ 213 465 988. Tues–Thurs
8pm–2am, Fri & Sat 7pm–3am. MAP PP.68–69,
POCKET MAP B11

A fine old bar with two rooms,
inexpensive drinks and laidback
sounds, usually world music.
Most Wednesdays there's a
band, often salsa/Brazilian.

MAHJONG

Rua da Atalaia 3 ☎ 213 421 039. Sun–Thurs
8pm–2am, Fri & Sat 8pm–3am. MAP PP.68–69,
POCKET MAP B12

At the bottom of the Bairro
Alto and traditionally a place to
start an evening before moving

on up. It's a great space, with
plain white tiles and a rough
wooden bar juxtaposed with
modern Chinese motifs – the
clientele are similarly eclectic.

MARIA CAXUXA

Rua da Barroca 6–12 ☎ 965 039 094. Daily
7pm–2am. MAP PP.68–69, POCKET MAP B12

This arty lounge-bar has plenty
of space for big sofas and
eclectic decor – including
record players and aged
machinery – though these get
lost in the crowds when the DJ
pumps up the volume as the
evening progresses.

PARK

Calçada do Combro 58 ☎ 215 914 011. Tues–
Sat 1pm–2am, Sun 1pm–8pm. MAP PP.68–69,
POCKET MAP A12

Reached via a poky entrance
inside a car park, this chic
rooftop bar comes as quite a
surprise. There are potted
plants and trees, great cocktails
and bar snacks, and a stunning
view across the river. At
weekends there are often guest
DJs and cultural events.

PAVILHÃO CHINÊS

Rua Dom Pedro V 89 ☎ 213 424 729. Daily
6pm–2am. MAP PP.68–69, POCKET MAP B10

Once a nineteenth-century tea
and coffee merchants' shop, this
is now a quirky bar set in a series
of comfy rooms, including a pool
room. Most are lined with
mirrored cabinets containing a
bizarre range of 4000 artefacts
from around the world, including
a cabinet of model trams. There's
waiter service and the usual
drinks are supplemented by a
long list of exotic cocktails.

PORTAS LARGAS

Rua da Atalaia 105 ☎ 218 466 379. Daily
6pm–2am. MAP PP.68–69, POCKET MAP B11

The bar's *portas largas* (big
doors) are usually thrown
wide open, inviting the

neighbouhood into this friendly black-and-white-tiled *adega* (wine cellar). There are cheapish drinks, music from fado to pop (sometimes live), and a young, mixed gay and straight clientele, which spills onto the streets.

SÉTIMO CÉU

Trav da Espera 54 ☎ 213 466 471. Mon–Sat 9pm–3am. MAP PP.68–69, POCKET MAP B12

An obligatory stop for gays and lesbians, who imbibe beers and *caipirinhas* served by the Brazilian owner. The great atmosphere spills out onto the street.

SOLAR DO VINHO DO PORTO

Rua de São Pedro de Alcântara 45 ☎ 213 475 707, ⓦ www.ivp.pt, Mon–Fri 11am–midnight, Sat 3pm–midnight. MAP PP.68–69, POCKET MAP B11

The eighteenth-century Palácio Ludovice is home to the Lisbon branch of the Port Wine Institute, responsible for promoting one of Portugal's most famous exports. Visitors are lured in with over three hundred types of port, starting at around €3 a glass and rising to some €25 for a glass of forty-year-old J.W. Burmester.

Drinks (as well as hams and cheeses) are served at low tables in the mansion's stylishly designed interior. The waiters are notoriously snooty but it's still a good place to kick off an evening.

Music venues

ALFACE HALL

Rua do Norte 96 ☎ 213 433 293. Daily 1pm–midnight. MAP PP.68–69, POCKET MAP C11

This quirky café-bar is in a former print works. Now part of a hostel and filled with retro chairs and artefacts, its high ceilings and comfy sofas make it an ideal place to hang out for live jazz and blues, daily from 9pm.

TASCA DO CHICO

Rua do Diário de Notícias 39 ☎ 965 059 670. Daily 7pm–2am. MAP PP.68–69, POCKET MAP B12

Atmospheric little bar filled with football scarves (a fine spot for a drink), which morphs into a very popular fado bar on Mondays and Wednesdays, when crowds pack in to hear moving fado from 8pm.

SOLAR DO VINHO DE PORTO

Estrela, Lapa and Santos

West of the Bairro Alto sits the leafy district of Estrela, best known for its gardens and enormous basílica. To the south lies opulent Lapa, Lisbon's diplomatic quarter, sheltering some of its top hotels. Sumptuous mansions and grand embassy buildings peer out majestically towards the Tejo. The superb Museu Nacional de Arte Antiga below here is Portugal's national gallery, while down on the riverfront, Santos is promoted as "the district of design" with some of the city's coolest shops.

BASÍLICA AND JARDIM DA ESTRELA

Largo da Estrela. Church Mon–Fri 7.30am–7.45pm, Sat 10am–6.30pm, Sun 3.30–7pm; closes for lunch 1–3pm. Free. Roof visits Mon–Sat 10am–6pm. €4. Tram #28 or #25. MAP OPPOSITE, POCKET MAP G6

The impressive Basílica da Estrela is a vast monument to late eighteenth-century Neoclassicism. Constructed by order of Queen Maria I (whose tomb lies within), and completed in 1790, its landmark white dome can be seen from much of the city. You can visit the flat roof (via 140 steep stone steps) for fine views over the western suburbs, and also walk round the inside of the dome to peer down at the church interior 25m below. Opposite is the **Jardim da Estrela** (daily; free), one of the city's most enjoyable gardens with a pond-side café and a well-equipped children's playground.

CEMITÉRIO DOS INGLESES

Rua São Jorge 6 ☎ 213 906 248. Mon–Fri 10am–1pm. Tram #28 or #25. MAP OPPOSITE, POCKET MAP G6

"The English Cemetery" is actually a cemetery for all Protestants, founded in 1717. Here, among the cypresses and tombs of various expatriates, lie the remains of Henry Fielding. He came to Lisbon hoping the climate would improve his failing health, but his inability to recuperate may have influenced his verdict on Lisbon as "the nastiest city in the world".

BASÍLICA DA ESTRELA

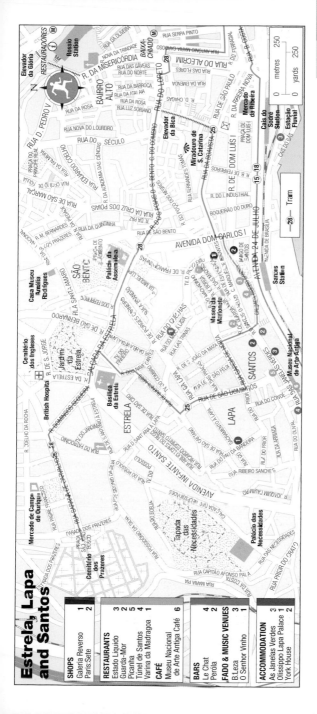

Estrela, Lapa and Santos

SHOPS	
Galeria Reverso	1
Paris-Sete	2

RESTAURANTS	
Estado Líquido	3
Guarda-Mor	5
Picanha	2
Túnel de Santos	4
Varina da Madragoa	1

CAFÉ	
Museu Nacional de Arte Antiga Café	6

BARS	
Le Chat	4
Pérola	2

FADO & MUSIC VENUES	
B.Leza	3
O Senhor Vinho	1

ACCOMMODATION	
As Janelas Verdes	3
Olissippo Lapa Palace	1
York House	2

LAPA

MAP P.79, POCKET MAP F7

From Estrela tram #25 skirts past the well-heeled district of Lapa on its way down to the waterfront. Lapa is the most desired address in the city and though it contains no sights as such, it is worth wandering around to admire the stunning mansions. A good route is to follow the tram tracks from Estrela and turn right into Rua do Sacramento à Lapa, past fantastic embassy buildings. Turn left into Rua do Pau da Bandeira past the *Olisippo Lapa Palace* hotel (if you have the funds, have a drink at the bar). From here, go left into Rua do Prior and right into Rua do Conde and it's a ten-minute walk downhill to the Museu Nacional de Arte Antiga (see below).

MUSEU NACIONAL DE ARTE ANTIGA

Rua das Janelas Verdes 95. Bus #760 from Praça da Figueira, #727 from Belém or a short walk from tram #25 ☎ 213 912 800, ⓦ www.mnarteantiga-ipmuseus.pt. Tues–Sun 10am–6pm. €6, free first Sun of the month.
MAP P.79, POCKET MAP G8

The Museu Nacional de Arte Antiga features the largest collection of Portuguese fifteenth- and sixteenth-century paintings in the country, European art from the fourteenth century to the present day and a rich display of applied art. All of this is well exhibited in a tastefully converted seventeenth-century palace once owned by the Marquês de Pombal. The museum uses ten "reference points" to guide you round the collection. The prinicipal highlight is **Nuno Gonçalves's altarpiece** dedicated to St Vincent (1467–70), a brilliantly marshalled composition depicting Lisbon's patron saint receiving homage from all ranks of its citizens, their faces appearing remarkably modern. The other main highlight is Hieronymus Bosch's stunningly gruesome *Temptation of St Anthony* in room 57 (don't miss the image on the back of the painting, showing the arrest of Christ). Elsewhere, seek out the altar panel depicting the *Resurrection* by Raphael; Francisco de Zurbarán's *The Twelve Apostles;* a small statue of a nymph by Auguste Rodin; and works by Dürer, Holbein, Cranach (particularly *Salome*),

MUSEU NACIONAL DE ARTE ANTIGA

Fragonard and Josefa de Óbidos, considered one of Portugal's greatest female painters.

The **Oriental art** collection shows how the Portuguese were influenced by overseas designs encountered during the sixteenth century. There is inlaid furniture from Goa, Turkish and Syrian *azulejos*, Qing Dynasty porcelain and a fantastic series of late sixteenth-century Japanese *namban* screens (room 14), depicting the Portuguese landing at Nagasaki. The Japanese regarded the Portuguese traders as southern barbarians (*namban*) with large noses – hence their Pinocchio-like features. The museum extends over the remains of the sixteenth-century St Albert monastery, most of which was razed during the 1755 earthquake, although its beautiful chapel can still be seen today, downstairs by the main entrance. Don't miss the garden café, either (see p.83).

SANTOS DISTRICT

displays and projections, masks from Africa and Asia, while the final room exhibits Wallace and Gromit-style plasticine figures with demonstrations on how they are manipulated for films.

SANTOS

MAP P.79, POCKET MAP G7

Santos was traditionally a run-down riverside area of factories and warehouses where people only ventured after dark because of its nightclubs. Over the years, artists and designers moved into the inexpensive and expansive warehouse spaces, and now Santos has a reputation as the city's designer heartland. Its riverside streets are not particularly alluring, but you can see many of the country's top designers showcasing their products in various shops and galleries. Fashionable bars and restaurants have followed in their wake, though the area around the Museu da Marioneta retains an earthy, villagey feel to its cobbled backstreets.

MUSEU DA MARIONETA

Rua da Esperança 146. Tram #25 then a short walk ☎ 213 942 810. ⓦ www.museuda marioneta.pt. Tues–Sun 10am–1pm & 2–6pm. €5, children €3, free Sun 10am–1pm. MAP P.79, POCKET MAP G7

Contemporary and historical puppets from around the world are displayed in this former eighteenth-century convent and demonstrated in a well-laid-out museum. Highlights include shadow puppets from Turkey and Indonesia, string marionettes, Punch and Judy-style puppets and almost life-sized, faintly disturbing modern figures by Portuguese puppeteer Helena Vaz, which are anything but cute. There are also video

Shops

GALERIA REVERSO

Rua da Esperança 59–61 ☎ 213 951 407.
Mon 2–6pm, Tues–Fri 11am–7pm. MAP P.79.
POCKET MAP H7

Jewellery workshop and gallery
managed by well-known
Portuguese designer Paula
Crespo, whose big, heavy
jewellery is eye-catching.
International designers also
feature, many using unusual
materials such as rubber and
wood, though to buy anything
you'll need a deep purse.

PARIS:SETE

Largo Vitorino Damásio 2 ☎ 213 933 170,
Ⓦ www.paris-sete.com. Mon–Fri 10am–7pm,
Sat 10.30am–2pm. MAP P.79. POCKET MAP H7

Bright, white space selling
designer furniture and curios,
with heavyweight names such
as Charles and Ray Eames
and Philippe Starck behind
some of them.

Restaurants

ESTADO LIQUIDO

Largo de Santos 5 ☎ 213 972 022, Ⓦ www
.estadoliquido.com. Mon–Fri 12.30–3pm &
8pm–midnight, Sat & Sun 1–3.30pm &
8pm–midnight. MAP P.79. POCKET MAP G7

Right on Santos' main square,
this is an ultrahip sushi
restaurant, with a downstairs
restaurant and fashionable
lounge room upstairs. You can
choose individual pieces of
sushi from around €7 or have
other mains from €25.

GUARDA-MOR

Rua do Guarda-Mor 8 ☎ 213 928 663.
Tues–Fri 12.30–3pm & 5.30pm–midnight, Sat
5.30pm–midnight. MAP P.79. POCKET MAP G7

One of Santos' more local
options serving great,
mid-priced dishes such as
pataniscas de bacalhau (dried

cod cakes), *açorda de gambas*
(prawns in bread sauce) and
gambas fritas com limão
(prawns fried in lemon). Also
has occasional live fado. Mains
from €14.

MERCADO DE CAMPO DE OURIQUE

Rua Coelho da Rocha ☎ 211 323 701. Mon–
Wed 10am–11pm, Thurs–Sat 10am–1am.
MAP P.79. POCKET MAP F6

This wonderful 1930s building
has been given a revamp and
now not only sells fish, fruit and
veg, but also shelters around
twenty *tasquinhas* (small food
stalls) serving pastries, sushi,
petiscos, burgers and sea food.
There are also bars (gin
cocktails, flavoured teas and the
like) and occasional live
entertainment in the evenings.

PICANHA

Rua das Janelas Verdes 96 ☎ 213 975 401.
Mon–Fri 12.30–3pm & 8–11pm, Sat & Sun
8–11pm. MAP P.79. POCKET MAP G8

This ornately-tiled restaurant
specializes in *picanha* (strips of
beef in garlic sauce) accompanied by black-eyed beans, salad
and potatoes. Great if this
appeals to you, since for a
fixed-price of around €20 you
can eat all you want; otherwise
forget it, as it's all that's on offer.

TÚNEL DE SANTOS

Largo de Santos 1 ☎ 912 151 850. Mon–Sat
noon–4am. MAP P.79. POCKET MAP G7

Lively, modern café-restaurant
with brick-vaulted ceilings and
outdoor seating facing the
square, attracting a young
crowd for inexpensive grills,
snacks and salads.

VARINA DA MADRAGOA

Rua das Madres 34 ☎ 213 965 533. Tues–Fri
12.30–3.30pm & 7.30–11.30pm, Sat
7.30–11.30pm. MAP P.79. POCKET MAP G7

A delightfully simple local that
has hosted the likes of fomer
US President Jimmy Carter

and Portuguese PM José Socrates – and it's easy to see why they liked it: a lovely, traditional restaurant with grape-motif *azulejos* on the walls and a menu featuring dishes such as *bacalhau*, trout and steaks. Desserts include a splendid almond ice cream with hot chocolate sauce. Mains from €10.

Café

MUSEU NACIONAL DE ARTE ANTIGA CAFÉ

Rua das Janelas Verdes 95 ☎ 213 912 800. Tues–Sun 10am–5.30pm. MAP P.79. POCKET MAP G8

There's no need to visit the museum to use its fantastic café – go in through the museum exit opposite Largo Dr J de Figueiredo and head to the basement. Lunches and drinks can be enjoyed in a superb garden studded with statues and overlooking Lisbon's docks.

Bars

LE CHAT

Jardim 9 de Abril ☎ 213 963 668. Mon–Sat 12.30pm–2am & Sun 12.30pm–midnight. MAP P.79, POCKET MAP F8

A modern, glass-sided café-bar adjacent to the Museu Nacional de Arte Antiga, *Le Chat* has a terrific terrace which gazes over the docks and Ponte 25 de Abril. Great at any time of the day, it's a particularly fine spot for a cocktail or sundowner.

PÉROLA

Calçada Ribeiro dos Santos 25 ☎ 917 745 516. Mon–Fri 8am–4am, Sat 11am–4am. MAP P.79, POCKET MAP G7

A small local bar given a makeover, with table football to play and a little back dining

LE CHAT

area. Most hole up in the front room for inexpensive drinks and good music.

Fado and music venues

B.LEZA

Cais da Ribeira Nova Armazém B ☎ 963 612 816. Wed–Sun 10.30pm–4am. MAP P.79. POCKET MAP A14

A great African club, with live music, poetry nights and occasional dance lessons on offer, though you'd be hard pushed to better the regulars.

O SENHOR VINHO

Rua do Meio à Lapa 18 ☎ 213 972 681. ⓦ www.srvinho.com. Mon–Sat 7.30pm–2am. MAP P.79, POCKET MAP G7

In the fashionable Madragoa district, this famous fado club features some of the best singers in Portugal, hence the high prices (around €50 a head). Reservations are advised.

Alcântara and the docks

Loomed over by the enormous Ponte 25 de Abril suspension bridge, Alcântara has a decidedly industrial hue, with a tangle of flyovers and cranes from the docks dominating the skyline. The area is well known for its nightlife, thanks mainly to its dockside warehouse conversions that shelter cafés, restaurants and clubs. It also hosts a couple of fine museums, both tipping their hats to Portugal's historic links with the Far East and there's an attractive riverside promenade. To get to the docks, take a train from Cais do Sodré to Alcântara-Mar or tram #15.

DOCA DE ALCÂNTARA

MAP BELOW, POCKET MAP F8

The earthy Doca de Alcântara remains the city's main harbour. After dark, the boat-bars and warehouse conversions come into their own; its clubs and bars attract an older, more moneyed crowd compared to the trendy Bairro Alto set who wouldn't be seen dead in these parts.

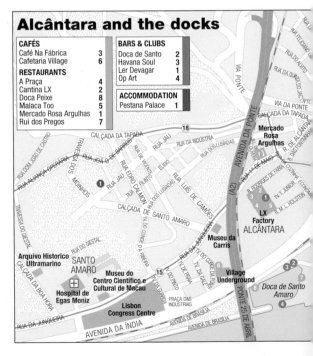

Alcântara and the docks

CAFÉS	
Café Na Fábrica	3
Cafetaria Village	6

RESTAURANTS	
A Praça	4
Cantina LX	2
Doca Peixe	8
Malaca Too	5
Mercado Rosa Argulhas	1
Rui dos Pregos	7

BARS & CLUBS	
Doca de Santo	2
Havana Soul	3
Ler Devagar	1
Op Art	4

ACCOMMODATION	
Pestana Palace	1

MUSEU DO ORIENTE

Avda de Brasília ☎ 213 585 200, ⊕ www
.museudooriente.pt. Tues–Sun 10am–6pm,
late opening Fri until 10pm. €6, free Fri
6–10pm. MAP BELOW, POCKET MAP E8

Owned by the powerful Orient
Foundation, this spacious
museum traces the cultural
links that Portugal has built up
with its former colonies in
Macao, India, East Timor and
other Asian countries. Housed
in an enormous 1930s Estado
Novo building, highlights of the
extensive collection include
valuable nineteenth-century
Chinese porcelain, an amazing
array of seventeenth-century
Chinese snuff boxes and, from
the same century, Japanese
armour and entire carved
pillars from Goa. The top floor
is given over to displays on the
Gods of Asia, featuring a bright
collection of religious costumes
and shrines used in Bali and

MUSEU DO ORIENTE

Vietnam together with Taoist
altars, statues of Buddha, some
fine Japanese Shinto masks and
Indonesian shadow puppets.
Vivid images of Hindu gods
Shiva, Ganesh the elephant
god and Kali the demon are
counterbalanced by some lovely
Thai amulets. There is also a
decent top floor restaurant.

DOCA DE SANTO AMARO

MAP PP.84–85, POCKET MAP D9

Just west of the Doca de
Alcântara lies the more
intimate Doca de Santo Amaro,
nestling right under the
humming traffic and rattling
trains crossing Ponte 25 de
Abril. This small, almost
completely enclosed marina is
filled with bobbing sailing
boats and lined with tastefully
converted warehouses. Its
international cafés and
restaurants are pricier than
usual for Lisbon but the
constant comings and goings of
the Tejo provide plenty of free
entertainment. Leaving Doca
de Santo Amaro at its western
side, you can pick up a pleasant
riverside path that leads all the
way to Belém (see p.86), twenty
minutes' walk away.

PONTE 25 DE ABRIL

MAP PP.84–85, POCKET MAP D9

Resembling the Golden Gate
Bridge in San Francisco, the
hugely impressive Ponte 25 de
Abril was opened in 1966 as a
vital link between Lisbon and
the southern banks of the Tejo.
Around 2.3km in length, the
main bridge rises to 70m above
the river, though its main pillars
are nearly 200m tall. It was
originally named Ponte de
Salazar after the dictatorial
prime minister who ruled
Portugal with an iron fist from
1932 to 1968, but took its
present name to mark the date
of the revolution that overthrew
Salazar's regime in 1974. You'll
pass over it if you take a bus or
train south of the Tejo. Driving
over it is pretty hairy, especially
on the lane made up of wire

mesh (it allows the bridge to expand) – it is both skiddy and see-through.

MUSEU DO CENTRO CIENTÍFICO E CULTURAL DE MACAU

Rua da Junqueira 30 ☏ 213 617 570, ⓦ www
.cccm.pt. Tues-Sun 10am-6pm. €3, free Sun
10am-2pm. MAP PP.84-85, POCKET MAP C9

This attractively laid-out museum is dedicated to Portugal's historical trading links with the Orient and, specifically, its former colony of Macao, which was handed back to Chinese rule in 1999. There are model boats and audio displays detailing early sea voyages, as well as various historic journals and artefacts, including a seventeenth-century portable wooden altar, used by travelling clergymen. Upstairs, exhibitions of Chinese art from the sixteenth to the nineteenth centuries show off ornate collections of porcelain, silverware and applied art, most notably an impressive array of opium pipes and ivory boxes.

MUSEU DA CARRIS

Rua 1º de Maio 101 ☏ 213 613 087, ⓦ www
.museu.carris.pt. Mon-Fri 10am-6pm,
Sat 10am-1pm & 2-6pm. €4. MAP PP.84-85,
POCKET MAP D8

This engagingly quirky and ramshackle museum traces the history of Lisbon's public transport, from the earliest trams and street lifts to the development of the metro. There are three zones, the first with evocative black-and-white photos, uniforms and models. You then hop on a real tram dating from 1901 which takes you to a warehouse filled with historic trams, and then on to another warehouse with ancient buses and models of metro trains. It's great fun for kids especially, who can

clamber on board and pretend to drive the vehicles. The bottom of the site also has the eye-catching Village Under-ground, a bizarre medley of old shipping containers and double-decker buses now given over to work spaces for writers and artists.

LX FACTORY

Rua Rodrigues Faria 103 ☏ 213 143 399,
ⓦ www.lxfactory.com. MAP PP.84-85,
POCKET MAP D8

Below Ponte 25 de Abril, this former industrial estate is now the place to test Lisbon's creative pulse. The factories and warehouses have turned into a mini district of workshops and studios for the city's go-getters, along with a series of superb boutiques, shops and cafés set in fashionably run-down urban spaces. Sunday is a good time to visit, with a lively flea market (noon-7pm) and many places open for brunch. Check the website for LX Factory's Open Days, when there are shows, live music and film screenings.

LER DEVAGAR, LX FACTORY

Cafés

CAFÉ NA FÁBRICA

LX Factory, Rua Rodrigues Faria 103 ☎ 214 010 807, ⓦ www.cafenafabrica.com. Mon–Fri 9am–8pm, Sat noon–7pm, Sun 10.30am–7pm. MAP PP.84–85, POCKET MAP D8

Set in a small but cosy wooden warehouse, this arty space is very popular for lunch, with wraps, quiches, baguettes and salads from around €7. There are also a few outdoor tables.

CAFETARIA VILLAGE

Village Underground, Rua 1° de Maio 103 ☎ 219 362 140. Tues–Sun noon–8pm (closes 6pm from Oct–Easter). MAP PP.64–85, POCKET MAP D9

Grab a sandwich, salad or dish of the day at the café inside Village Underground (see p.87) which is inside an old double-decker bus. There are tables inside or out, where you can sit with Lisbon's creative set.

Restaurants

A PRAÇA

LX Factory, Edifício H, Espaço 001 ☎ 210 991 792, ⓦ www.restaurantepraca.com. Tues–Sun noon–3pm & 8–11.30pm. MAP PP.84–85, POCKET MAP D8

One of the larger restaurants in LX Factory, a hip spot with an open kitchen serving a range of dishes including pasta, steaks and seafood from €12–15. It also does good cocktails.

CANTINA LX

LX Factory, Rua Rodrigues Faria 103 ☎ 213 628 239. Mon noon–3pm, Tues–Sat noon–3pm & 7.30pm–midnight, Sun noon–3pm. MAP PP.84–85, POCKET MAP D8

Upcycled furniture and bench-like tables in a spacious former warehouse make this a hip spot. Great breakfasts, snacks and daily specials which usually focus on healthy salads from around €10.

DOCA PEIXE

Armazém 14, Doca de Santo Amaro ☎ 213 973 556, ⓦ www.docapeixe.com. Daily 12.30–11.30pm. MAP PP.84–85, POCKET MAP D9

You'll need a deep wallet to eat at this fish restaurant (mains from €16), but with a counter groaning under the weight of fresh fish, you won't leave disappointed. They also serve a great prawn curry and sublime lobster rice with clams.

MALACA TOO

LX Factory, Rua Rodrigues Faria 103, Edifício G-03 ☎ 213 477 082. Daily noon–3pm & 8pm–3am. MAP PP.84–85, POCKET MAP D8

This fantastic space has tables wedged between giant old printing presses – a surprising backdrop for fresh, oriental cuisine ranging from wanton soup and green curries to fresh fish, from around €12.

MERCADO ROSA ARGULHAS

Mercado Rosa Agulhas, Rua Leão de Oliveira,
Loja 25 ☎ 213 649 113. Tues–Sat noon–3pm
& 7–10pm, Sun noon–3pm. MAP PP.84–85,
POCKET MAP D8

On three floors by the market
building – and Lisbon's markets
are always worth a call – this is
a great place to have a hearty
meal. The ingredients don't have
far to travel: the fish and
vegetables are day fresh, and
there's a long list of grilled meats
and seafood, including a fine
seafood pasta. Mains €12–14.

RUI DOS PREGOS

Passeio Doca de Santo Amaro ☎ 967 723 483.
Tues–Sun noon–2am. MAP PP.84–85, POCKET MAP D9

One of the less pricey options
set to one side of the docks,
with appealing outdoor tables.
The speciality here is *pregos*
(beef sandwiches), with
different varieties from €8.

Bars and clubs

DOCA DE SANTO

Armazém CP, Doca de Santo Amaro ☎ 213
963 522. Mon–Thurs & Sun 9am–midnight, Fri
& Sat 9am–2am. MAP PP.84–85, POCKET MAP D8

CANTINA LX

Though it's located slightly
away from the river, this
palm-fringed venue is worth
seeking out; there's an enticing
cocktail bar on the esplanade,
while the restaurant inside
serves well-priced modern
Portuguese food (grilled fish
and meats with pasta or
couscous). From €10.

HAVANA SOUL

Armazém 5, Doca de Santo Amaro ☎ 213 979
893, ⓦ www.barhavana.pt. Daily noon–4am.
MAP PP.84–85, POCKET MAP D9

Cuban-themed music bar with
wicker chairs and Latin music
in a lovely position overlooking
the marina. It also does
moderately-priced salads and
snacks as well as occasional
club nights.

LER DEVAGAR

LX Factory, Rua Rodrigues Faria 103, Edifício
G-03 ☎ 213 259 992, ⓦ www.lerdevagar.com.
Mon noon–9pm, Tues–Thurs noon–midnight,
Fri & Sat noon–2am, Sun 11am–9pm.
MAP PP.84–85, POCKET MAP D8

Primarily a wonderful arts
bookshop, with shelves
reaching an old printing press,
this also has a corner café-bar,
a great place to sample
Portuguese wines by the glass.
It also hosts exhibits and
occasional live music.

OP ART

Doca de Santo Amaro ☎ 213 956 787,
ⓦ www.opartcafe.com. Tues–Fri & Sun
3pm–2am, Sat 3pm–6am. MAP PP.84–85,
POCKET MAP D9

Set in splendid isolation on the
fringes of the Tejo, this small
glass pavilion morphs from a
minimalist restaurant serving
moderately priced grills into a
groovy evening bar. After dusk,
the volume pumps up and it
turns into more of a club. In
summer, you can sprawl on the
dockside beanbags and gaze
over the river.

Belém and Ajuda

With its maritime history and attractive riverside location, Belém (pronounced ber-layng) is understandably one of Lisbon's most popular suburbs. It was from Belém that Vasco da Gama famously set sail for India in 1497 and returned a year later. The monastery subsequently built here – the Mosteiro dos Jerónimos – stands as a testament to his triumphant discovery of a sea route to the Orient, which initiated the beginning of a Portuguese golden age. Along with the monastery and the landmark Torre de Belém, the suburb boasts a group of small museums including the fantastic Berardo Collection of modern art. Just to the northeast of Belém is Ajuda, famed for its palace and ancient botanical gardens. Higher still lies the extensive parkland of Monsanto, Lisbon's largest green space.

PRAÇA DO IMPÉRIO

MAP PP92–93, POCKET MAP C4

The formal walkways and gardens that make up Praça do Império are laid out over Belém's former beach. It's a popular spot, especially on Saturday mornings, when there are often weddings taking place at the monastery, whose photocalls invariably spill out into the square. The seventeenth-century buildings along Rua Vieira Portuense are now mostly restaurants with outdoor seating; as a rule, the further east you head, the better value they become.

JARDIM DO ULTRAMAR AND PRESIDÊNCIA DA REPÚBLICA

Garden entrance on Calçada do Galvão ☎ 213 609 660, ⬤ www2.iict.pt. Daily: May–Aug 10am–8pm; Sept–April 10am–dusk. €2. MAP PP92–93, POCKET MAP C4

The leafy Jardim do Ultramar is an oasis of hothouses, ponds and towering palms, a lovely place for a shady walk. In the southeastern corner lies the President's official residence, the pink Presidência da República, which opens its state rooms for guided visits on Saturdays (entrance on Praça Afonso de Albuquerque; Sat

Belém transport

You can reach Belém on tram #15 (signed Algés), which runs from Praça da Figueira via Praça do Comércio (20min). Ask at the ticket offices of the main sites about combined tickets that can save money on entry to the main attractions, which all attract long queues in the summer. You can also take a 45-minute Yellowbus minibus tour (June–Sept roughly every 30min, 10am–6.30pm; Oct–May every hour Mon–Fri, from 10am–noon & 2–5pm, every 30min Sat & Sun; €9, valid 24 hours), departing from in front of the Mosteiro dos Jerónimos, which goes up to the palace at Ajuda and back via the Torre de Belém. Alternatively, hire bikes (Mon–Fri 10.30am–8pm, 7pm in winter, Sat & Sun 9.30am–8pm, 7pm in winter, €4.50/1hr; ⬤ www.belembike .com) from a kiosk just east of the Museu da Electricidade (see p.95)

MOSTEIRO DOS JERÓNIMOS

10.30am–4.30pm, €5; ⓦ www
.museu.presidencia.pt).

MUSEU DE ARTE POPULAR

Avda de Brasília ☎ 213 011 282, ⓦ www
.map.imc-ip.pt. Wed–Fri 10am–6pm, Sat &
Sun 10am–1pm & 2–6pm. €2.50, free first
Sun of the month. MAP PP92–93, POCKET MAP D5
In a space which feels slightly
too large for its exhibits, this
charming museum chronicles
Portugal's folk art, from
beautiful wood and cork toys to
ceramics, rugs and fascinating
traditional costumes, including
amazing cloaks from the
Trás-os-Montes region.

MOSTEIRO DOS JERÓNIMOS

Praça do Império ☎ 213 620 034, ⓦ www
.mosteirojeronimos.pt. Tues–Sun: May–Sept
10am–6.30pm; Oct–April 10am–5.30pm;
restricted access on Sat mornings and during
Mass. €10. MAP PP92–93, POCKET MAP C4
If there's one building that
symbolizes the Golden Age of
the Portuguese discoveries, it's
the Mosteiros dos Jerónimos,
which is also considered to be
the first ever Manueline
building. Now a UNESCO
World Heritage Site, the
monastery and its adjacent
church were built to fulfill a
promise that Portugal's king,
Dom Manuel made, should
Vasco da Gama return safely
from his inaugural voyage to
India in 1498. Construction

began in 1502 under the
architect Diogo de Boitaca.
   Appropriately, Vasco da
Gama's tomb now lies just
inside the fantastically
embellished entrance to the
church. Crowned by an
elaborate medley of statues,
including Henry the Navigator,
the 32-metre-high entrance was
designed by the Spaniard João
de Castilho, who took over the
building of the church in 1517.
The interior is even more
dazzling, displaying the
maritime influences typical of
Manueline architecture. The
church also contains the tomb
of Luís de Camões (1527–
1570), Portugal's greatest poet
and recorder of the discoveries,
alongside the tombs of former
presidents and dignataries.
   Equally impressive is the
adjacent monastery, gathered
round sumptuously vaulted
cloisters with nautical symbols
carved into the honey-coloured
limestone. You can still see the
twelve niches where navigators
stopped for confessionals before
their voyages of exploration,
until the Hieronymite monks
were forced out during the
dissolution of 1833. In 2007, the
monastery was again influential
in blessing future trade: the
Treaty of Lisbon was signed
here to cement the format of
the European Union.

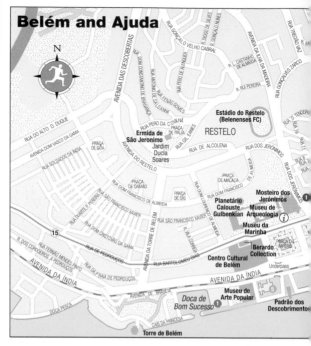

Belém and Ajuda

MUSEU DE ARQUEOLOGIA

Praça do Império ☎ 213 620 000, 🌐 www
.museuarqueologia.pt. Tues–Sun 10am–6pm.
€5, free first Sun of the month. MAP ABOVE,
POCKET MAP C4

Housed in a neo-Manueline
extension to the monastery
added in 1850, the archeology
museum has a small section on
Egyptian antiquities dating
from 6000 BC, but concentrates
on Portuguese archeological
finds. It's a sparse collection
reprieved by coins and
jewellery through the ages, and
a few fine Roman mosaics.

MUSEU DA MARINHA

Praça do Império ☎ 213 620 019, 🌐 www
.museu.marinha.pt. Tues–Sun: May–Sept
10am–6pm; Oct–April 10am–5pm. €6, free
first Sun of the month. MAP ABOVE, POCKET MAP B4

In the west wing of the
monastery extension is an
absorbing and gargantuan
maritime museum, packed not
only with models of ships, naval
uniforms and artefacts from
Portugal's Oriental colonies, but
also with real vessels – among
them fishing boats and
sumptuous state barges, plus
early seaplanes. Much of the
collection comes from that of
King Luís I (1861–1889), a keen
oceanographer.

CENTRO CULTURAL DE BELÉM

Praça do Império ☎ 213 612 400, 🌐 www.ccb
.pt. MAP ABOVE, POCKET MAP B4

The stylish, modern, pink
marble Centro Cultural de
Belém was built to host Lisbon's
1992 presidency of the
European Union. It's now one
of the city's main cultural
centres, containing the Berardo
Collection (see opposite) and
hosting regular photography
and art exhibitions, as well as
concerts and shows.

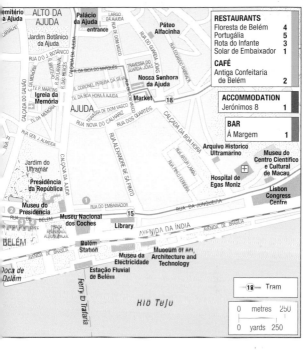

RESTAURANTS

Floresta de Belém	4
Portugália	5
Rota do Infante	3
Solar de Embaixador	1

CAFÉ

| Antiga Confeitaria de Belém | 2 |

ACCOMMODATION

| Jerónimos 8 | 1 |

BAR

| Á Margem | 1 |

| 18 | Tram |

| 0 | metres | 250 |
| 0 | yards | 250 |

RIO TEJO

BERARDO COLLECTION

Entrance via Centro Cultural de Belém, Praça do Império ☎ 213 612 878, ⓦ www .museuberardo.pt. Tues-Sun 10am–7pm. Free.
MAP ABOVE, POCKET MAP B4

As impressive as Belém's historical monuments is this unique collection of modern art amassed by wealthy Madeiran Joe Berardo, Portugal's answer to Charles Saatchi or François Pinault. You can enjoy some of the world's top modern artists, though not all of the vast collection is on display at the same time. Depending on when you visit, you may see Eric Fischl's giant panels of sunbathers; Andy Warhol's distinctive *Judy Garland*; and Chris Ofili's *Adoration of Captain Shit*, made with genuine dung. Portugal's Paula Rego is well represented – *The Past and Present* and *The Barn* are particularly strong. Francis Bacon, David Hockney, Picasso, Míro, Man Ray, Max Ernst and Mark Rothko also feature, along with various video artists.

MARCEL DUCHAMP SCULPTURE AT THE BERARDO COLLECTION

BELÉM AND AJUDA

PADRÃO DOS DESCOBRIMENTOS

Avda de Brasília, reached via an underpass beneath the Avda da Índia ☎ 213 031 950, ⓦ www.padraodescobrimentos.egeac.pt. Daily: March–Sept 10am–7pm; Oct–Feb 10am–6pm. €4. MAP PP.92–93, POCKET MAP C5

The Padrão dos Descobrimentos (Monument to the Discoveries) is a 54m-high, caravel-shaped slab of concrete erected in 1960 to commemorate the 500th anniversary of the death of Henry the Navigator. A large and detailed statue of Henry appears at the head of a line of statues that feature King Alfonso V, Luís de Camões, Vasco de Gama and other Portuguese heroes. Inside is a small exhibition space which often features displays on Lisbon's history – the entrance fee also includes a ride in the lift providing fine views of the Tejo and the Torre de Belém. Just in front of the monument, tourists pose on the marble pavement decorated with a map of the world charting the routes taken by the great Portuguese explorers.

TORRE DE BELÉM

Avda de Brasília ☎ 213 620 034. Tues–Sun: May–Sept 10am–6.30pm; Oct–April 10am–5.30pm. €6, free first Sun of the month. MAP PP.92–93, POCKET MAP A5

Reached via a narrow walkway and jutting into the river, the impressive Torre de Belém (Tower of Belém) has become an iconic symbol of Lisbon. It is fashioned in the Manueline style that was prominent during the reign of Manuel, its windows and stairways embellished with arches and decorative symbols representing Portugal's explorations into the New World. Built as a fortress to defend the mouth of the River Tejo, it took five years to complete, though when it opened in 1520 it would have been near the centre of the river – the earthquake of 1755 shifted the river's course. Today, visitors are free to explore the tower's various levels, which include a terrace facing the river from where artillery would have been fired. You can then climb a very steep spiral staircase up four levels – each with a slightly different framed view of the river – to a top terrace where you get a blowy panorama of Belém. You can also duck into the dungeons, a low-ceilinged room used to store gunpowder; these were also utilized notoriously by Dom Miguel to lock up political prisoners in the nineteenth century.

PADRÃO DOS DESCOBRIMENTOS

TORRE DE BELÉM

The quirky red-brick Museu da Electricidade (Electricity Museum) is housed in an early twentieth-century electricity generating station. The highlights include a series of enormous generators, steam turbines and winches; it also hosts regular art and technology exhibitions. The impressively futuristic building alongside is the **Museum of Art, Architecture and Technology**, designed by British architect Amanda Levete. Its expansive interior hosts temporary exhibitions, or you can just walk over the exterior and down a staircase that leads to the Tagus.

MUSEU DOS COCHES

Avda Índia 136 and Praça Afonso de Albuquerque ☎ 213 610 850, ⓦ www .museudoscoches.pt. Tues–Sun 10am–6pm. Museu dos Coches €6, Royal Riding School €4, both €8, free 1st Sun of each month. MAP PP.92-93, POCKET MAP D4

Housed in a vast contemporary building, the Museu dos Coches (Coach Museum) contains one of the world's largest collections of carriages and saddlery, including a rare sixteenth-century coach designed for King Felipe I. Heavily gilded, ornate and often beautifully painted, the royal carriages, sedan chairs and children's cabriolets dating from the sixteenth to nineteenth centuries, contrast with the stark modern building, which gives great views over Belém and the river. More coaches from the collection are on display in the former Royal Riding School across the road, though it's only really the historic building itself that warrants the additional entrance fee.

MUSEU DA ELECTRICIDADE

Avda de Brasília ☎ 210 028 130, ⓦ www .fundacaoedp.pt. Tues–Sun 10am–6pm. Free. MAP PP.92-93, POCKET MAP D4

PALÁCIO DA AJUDA

Largo da Ajuda. Tram #18 from Praça do Comércio or bus #729 from Belém ☎ 213 620 264, ⓦ www.palacioajuda.pt. Mon, Tues & Thurs–Sun 10am–6pm. €6, free first Sun of the month. MAP PP.92-93, POCKET MAP D2

This massive nineteenth-century palace sits on a hillside above Belém. Construction began in 1802, but was left incomplete when João VI and the royal family fled to Brazil to escape Napoleon's invading army in 1807. The original plans were therefore never fulfilled, though the completed section was used as a royal residence after João returned from exile in 1821. The crashingly tasteless decor was commissioned by the nineteenth-century royal, Dona Maria II (João's granddaughter), and gives an insight into the opulent life the royals lived. The Queen's bedroom comes complete with a polar bear-skin rug, while the throne and ballroom are impressive for their sheer size and extravagance. The highly ornate banqueting hall, full of crystal chandeliers, is also breathtaking.

JARDIM BOTÂNICO DA AJUDA

Entrance on Calçada da Ajuda and Calçada do Galvão ☏ 213 622 503, Ⓦ www .jardimbotanicodaajuda.com. Daily: May–Sept 9am–8pm; Oct–April 9am–6pm. €2. MAP PP.92–93, POCKET MAP C2

A classic example of formal Portuguese gardening, this is one of the city's oldest and most interesting botanical gardens. Commissioned by the Marquês de Pombal and laid out in 1768, it was owned by the royal family until the birth of the Republic in 1910, then substantially restored in the 1990s. The garden is divided into eight parts planted with species from around the world, arranged around terraces, statues and fountains, much of it with lovely views over the river.

PÁTEO ALFACINHA

Rua do Guarda Jóias 44 ☏ 213 628 258, Ⓦ www.pateoalfacinha.com. MAP PP.92–93, POCKET MAP D2

Just five minutes' walk from the Palácio da Ajuda, it is worth seeking out this highly picturesque *páteo* – a renovated cluster of traditional nineteenth-century Lisbon houses gathered round a central patio. These were common in the days when families lived in tight-knit communities who looked after and traded with each other. Today the houses only come alive for special events and private parties, often at weekends, though there are two decent restaurants (closed Sundays), one which is open in summer and the other in winter.

PARQUE FLORESTAL DE MONSANTO

Bus #729 from Ajuda or Belém. MAP PP.92–93, POCKET MAP E2

The extensive hillside Parque Florestal de Monsanto – home to the city's main and well-equipped campsite (Ⓦ www.lisboacamping.com) – is known as "Lisbon's lungs" though it used to be infamous for the prostitutes who worked here until the Mayor of Lisbon bought a house nearby in 2003. Suddenly the park was given a new lease of life and the hookers have been replaced by horse-and-trap rides to its splendid viewpoints. At weekends in summer the area is completely traffic-free and pop concerts are often laid on, usually free of charge.

Restaurants

FLORESTA DE BELÉM

Praça Afonso de Albuquerque 1a ☎ 213 636
307, ⓦ www.florestadebelem.com. Tues–Sat
11am–4pm & 6.30pm–midnight, Sun
11am–4pm. MAP PP.92–93, POCKET MAP C4

On the corner with Rua Vieira
Portuense, this attracts a largely
Portuguese clientele, especially
for lunch at the weekend. Great
salads, grills and fresh fish from
around €7–9, served inside or
on a sunny outdoor terrace.

PORTUGÁLIA

Avda de Brasilia Edif. Espelho d'Água
☎ 213 032 700, ⓦ www.portugalia.pt. Daily
noon–midnight. MAP PP.92–93, POCKET MAP C4

Marooned on a little island in
an artificial lake facing the
Padrão dos Descobrimentos,
this glass-fronted restaurant,
which is part of a popular chain,
has a serene position. Dishes
including *bitoques* (small steaks)
from €10 and a wonderful
gambas à brás (prawns with
stick potatoes and onions). Most
mains are €12–16.

ROTA DO INFANTE

Rua Vieira Portuense 10–14 ☎ 213 646 787.
Daily noon–3pm & 7.30–11pm, closed Mon
Oct–April. MAP PP.92–93, POCKET MAP C4

One of the best-value places in
this pretty row of buildings
facing the greenery of Praça do
Império. Decently priced fish
and meat from around €7–11,
with outdoor seats under
fragrant orange trees.

SOLAR DE EMBAIXADAR

Rua do Embaixador 210–212 ☎ 213 625 111.
Mon & Wed–Sun noon–3pm & 7–11pm.
MAP PP.92–93, POCKET MAP D4

Close to the Coach Museum,
this homely restaurant serves
favourites such as *bitoque* (thin
steak), *alheira* sausages and
fresh fish from €7–9, with a TV
in the corner for company.

Café

ANTIGA CONFEITARIA DE BELÉM

Rua de Belém 84–92 ⓦ www.pasteisdebelem
.pt. Daily 8am–midnight, Oct–May closes
11pm. MAP PP.92–93, POCKET MAP C4

No visit to Belém is complete
without a coffee and hot *pastel
de nata* (custard-cream tart)
liberally sprinkled with *canela*
(cinnamon) in this cavernous,
tiled pastry shop and café,
which has been serving them up
since 1837. The place positively
heaves, especially at weekends,
but there's usually space to sit
down in its warren of rooms.

Bar

Á MARGEM

Doca do Bom Sucesso ☎ 916 588 859, ⓦ www
.amargem.com. Mon–Thurs 10am–10pm, Fri &
Sat 10am–2am. MAP PP.92–93, POCKET MAP B5

Chic and minimalist café-bar
with stunning views across the
river – tables spill out onto the
waterfront. Sarnies from €7 plus
tapas, salads and a good list of
cocktails and wines. It's near the
brick-striped stumpy lighthouse.

ANTIGA CONFEITARIA DE BELÉM

Avenida, Parque Eduardo VII and the Gulbenkian

Lisbon's main avenue, Avenida da Liberdade (simply known as "Avenida"), links the centre with its principal park, Parque Eduardo VII, best known for its views and enormous hothouses. The avenue, together with its side streets, was once home to statesmen and public figures. On its western side is the historic Praça das Amoreiras, the finishing point of the massive Águas Livres aqueduct. Here you'll find the Casa Museu Siznes-Viera da Silva, a collection of works by two artists heavily influenced by Lisbon. Northwest of the park, the Fundação Calouste Gulbenkian is undoubtedly Portugal's premier cultural centre, featuring one of Europe's richest art collections. Art-lovers have a further attraction to the east, where you can view the historic paintings and objects in the Casa Museu Dr Anastácio Gonçalves. Just north of here is the bullring at Campo Pequeno, while east lies the city's zoo.

AVENIDA DA LIBERDADE

MAP PP.100–101, POCKET MAP J5

The 1.3km, palm-lined Avenida da Liberdade is still much as poet Fernando Pessoa described it: "the finest artery in Lisbon… full of trees… small gardens, ponds, fountains, cascades and statues". It was laid out in 1882 as the city's main north–south avenue and has several appealing outdoor cafés under the shade of trees that help cushion the roar of

AVENIDA DA LIBERDADE

the passing traffic. Some of the avenue's original nineteenth-century mansions remain, though most have been replaced by modern buildings. The upper end of the avenue (Lisbon's most expensive real estate) houses many of the city's designer shops and ends in a swirl of traffic at the landmark roundabout of Praça Marquês de Pombal, also known as Rotunda.

PARQUE MAYER

MAP PP.100–101, POCKET MAP J5

Opened in 1922 as an "entertainment precinct" when theatres were all the rage, the run-down Parque Mayer is still one of the capital's main destinations for theatregoers. The latest of many plans for redevelopment may see it turned into a Cultural Village, complete with a School of Dance, Toy Museum and cinema, and the possible renovation of the **Teatro Capitólio**, Portugal's first great Modernist structure.

CASA MUSEU MEDEIROS E ALMEIDA

Rua Rosa Araújo 41 ☎ 213 547 892, ⊕ www .casa-museumedeirosealmeida.pt. Mon–Fri 1–5.30pm, Sat 10am–5.30pm. €5, free Sat 10am–1pm. MAP PP.100–101, POCKET MAP H5
This excellent museum was the home of the industrialist, philanthropist and art collector António Medeiros until his death in 1986. Today it serves as a showcase for his priceless series of artefacts. His collection of 225 Chinese porcelain items (some 2000 years old), sixteenth- to nineteenth-century watches, and English and Portuguese silverware are considered the most valuable in the world. Other highlights include glorious eighteenth-century *azulejos* in the Sala de Lago, a

MURAL, PARQUE MAYER

room complete with large water fountains; and a rare seventeenth-century clock, made for Queen Catherine of Bragança and mentioned by Samuel Pepys in his diary.

PRAÇA DAS AMOREIRAS

MAP PP.100–101, POCKET MAP G5

One of Lisbon's most tranquil squares, Praça das Amoreiras – complete with kids' play area – is dominated on its western side by the Águas Livres aqueduct (see p.102), with a chapel wedged into its arches.

On the south side the **Mãe d'Água** cistern (☎ 218 100 215; Tues–Sat 10am–12.30pm & 1.30–5.30pm; €5) marks the end of the line for the aqueduct. Built between 1746 and 1834, the castellated stone building contains a reservoir that once supplied the city. The structure nowadays hosts occasional temporary art exhibitions. Head to the back where there are stairs leading on to the roof for great views over the city. Back on the square, the little kiosk café is a popular spot for a coffee or beer and also hosts occasional art exhibits.

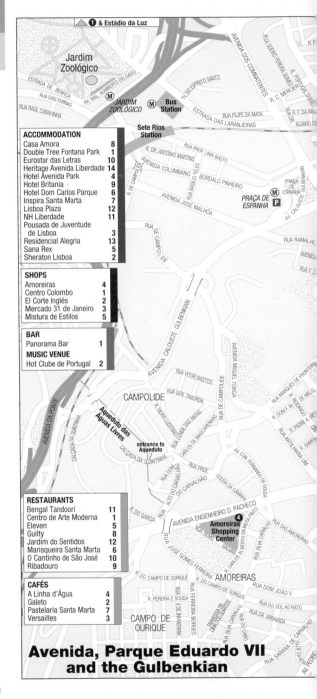

△ ❶ & Estádio da Luz

Jardim Zoológico

ACCOMMODATION

Casa Amora	8
Double Tree Fontana Park	1
Eurostar das Letras	10
Heritage Avenida Liberdade	14
Hotel Avenida Park	4
Hotel Britania	9
Hotel Dom Carlos Parque	6
Inspira Santa Marta	7
Lisboa Plaza	12
NH Liberdade	11
Pousada de Juventude de Lisboa	3
Residencial Alegria	13
Sana Rex	5
Sheraton Lisboa	2

SHOPS

Amoreiras	4
Centro Colombo	1
El Corte Inglés	2
Mercado 31 de Janeiro	3
Mistura de Estilos	5

BAR

Panorama Bar	1

MUSIC VENUE

Hot Clube de Portugal	2

RESTAURANTS

Bengal Tandoori	11
Centro de Arte Moderna	1
Eleven	5
Guilty	8
Jardim do Sentidos	12
Marisqueira Santa Marta	6
O Cantinho de São José	10
Ribadouro	9

CAFÉS

A Linha d'Água	4
Galeto	2
Pastelaria Santa Marta	7
Versailles	3

Avenida, Parque Eduardo VII and the Gulbenkian

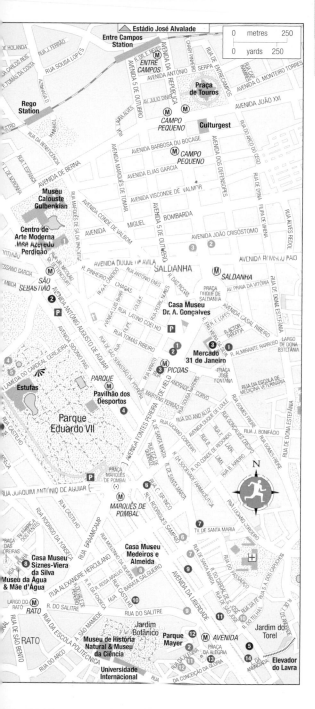

CASA MUSEU SIZNES-VIERA DA SILVA

Praça das Amoreiras 56–58 ☎ 213 880 044, ⓦ www.fasvs.pt. Tues–Sun 10am–6pm. €5, free first Sun of the month. MAP PP:100–101, POCKET MAP G5

Casa Museu Siznes-Viera da Silva is a small but highly appealing gallery dedicated to the works of two painters and the artists who have been influenced by them. Arpad Siznes (1897–1985) was a Hungarian-born artist and friend of Henri Matisse and Pierre Bonnard, among others. While in Paris in 1928 he met the Portuguese artist Maria Helena Viera da Silva (1908–92), whose work was influenced by the surrealism of Joan Miró and Max Ernst, with both of whom she was good friends. Siznes and Viera da Silva married in 1930 and, in 1936, both exhibited in Lisbon, where they briefly lived, before eventually settling in France. The foundation shows the development of the artists' works, with Viera da Silva's more abstract, subdued paintings contrasting with flamboyant Siznes, some of whose paintings show the clear influence of Miró.

AQUEDUTO DAS ÁGUAS LIVRES

Entrance on Calçada da Quintinha 6. Bus #712/#758 from Amoreiras ☎ 218 100 215. March–Oct Tues–Sat 10am–5.30pm. €3. MAP PP:100–101, POCKET MAP F4

The towering Aqueduto das Águas Livres (Free Waters Aqueduct) was opened in 1748, bringing a reliable source of safe drinking water to the city for the first time. Stretching for 60km (most of it underground), the aqueduct stood firm during the 1755 earthquake though it later gained a more notorious reputation thanks to one Diogo Alves, a nineteenth-century serial killer who threw his victims off the top – a seventy-metre drop. It is possible to walk across a 1.5km section of the aqueduct, though you'll need a head for heights. The walkable section is accessed off a quiet residential street through a small park in Campolide, 1km north of Praça das Amoreiras.

FUNDAÇÃO CALOUSTE GULBENKIAN

Avda de Berna 45a ☎ 217 823 000, ⓦ www .gulbenkian.pt. MAP PP:100–101, POCKET MAP H2

Set in extensive grounds, the Fundação Calouste Gulbenkian was set up by the Armenian oil magnate Calouste Gulbenkian (see box opposite) whose legendary art-market coups included the acquisition of works from the Hermitage in St Petersburg. Today the Gulbenkian Foundation has a multi-million-dollar budget sufficient to finance work in all spheres of Portuguese cultural life. In this low-rise 1960s complex alone, it runs an orchestra, three concert halls and an attractive open-air amphitheatre.

AQUEDUTO DAS ÁGUAS LIVRES

MUSEU CALOUSTE GULBENKIAN

Avda de Berna 45a ☎ 217 823 000, Ⓦ www.
museu.gulbenkian.pt. Mon & Wed–Sun
10am–6pm. €5, free Sun, combined ticket with
Centro de Arte Moderna €8. MAP PP.100–101.
POCKET MAP H2

The Museu Calouste Gulbenkian covers virtually every
phase of Eastern and Western
art. The small Egyptian room
displays art from the Old
Kingdom (c.2700 BC) up to the
Roman period. Fine Roman
statues, silver and glass, and
gold jewellery from ancient
Greece follow. The Islamic arts
are magnificently represented
by a variety of ornamental
texts, opulently woven carpets,
glassware and Turkish tiles.
There is also porcelain from
China, and beautiful Japanese
prints and lacquerwork.

European art includes work
from all the major schools. The
seventeenth-century collection
yields Peter Paul Rubens'
graphic *The Love of the Centaurs*
(1635) and Rembrandt's *Figure
of an Old Man*. Featured
eighteenth-century works
include those by Jean-Honoré
Fragonard and Thomas
Gainsborough – in particular
the stunning *Portrait of Mrs
Lowndes-Stone*. The big names

MUSEU CALOUSTE GULBENKIAN

of nineteenth- to twentieth
century France – Manet, Monet,
Degas, Millet and Renoir – are
all represented, along with John
Sargent and Turner's vivid
Wreck of a Transport Ship
(1810). Elsewhere you'll find
Sèvres porcelain and furniture
from the reigns of Louis XV and
Louis XVI. The last room
features an amazing collection
of Art Nouveau jewellery by
René Lalique. Don't miss the
fantastical *Peitoral-libélula*
(Dragonfly breastpiece) brooch,
decorated with enamelwork,
gold and diamonds.

AVENIDA, PARQUE EDUARDO VII AND THE GULBENKIAN

Calouste Gulbenkian

Calouste Sarkis Gulbenkian (1869–1955) was the Roman Abramovich of
his era, making his millions from oil but investing in the world's best
art rather than footballers. Born of wealthy Armenian parents in
Istanbul in 1869, he followed his father into the oil industry and eventually
moved to England. After the Russian Revolution of 1917 he bought works
from the Leningrad Hermitage. During World War II, his Turkish background
made him unwelcome in Britain and Gulbenkian auctioned himself to
whoever would have him. Portugal bid an aristocratic palace (a marquês was
asked to move out) and tax exemption, to acquire one of the most important
cultural patrons of the century. From 1942 to his death in 1955, he
accumulated one of the best private art collections in the world. His dying
wish was that all of his collection should be displayed in one place, and this
was granted in 1969 with the opening of the Museu Calouste Gulbenkian.

CENTRO DE ARTE MODERNA JOSÉ AZEREDO PERDIGÃO

Main entrance on Rua Dr Nicolau de Bettencourt ☎ 217 823 474, Ⓦ www.cam .gulbenkian.pt. Mon & Wed–Sun 10am–5.45pm. €5, free Sun, combined ticket with Museu Calouste Gulbenkian €8. MAP PP.100–101, POCKET MAP H2

The Centro de Arte Moderna, part of the Gulbenkian foundation (see p.103), features pop art, installations and sculptures – some witty, some baffling, but all thought-provoking. Most of the big names on the twentieth-century Portuguese scene are included, including portraits and sketches by Almada Negreiros (1873–1970), the founder of *modern-ismo*; the bright Futurist colours of Amadeu de Sousa Cardoso; and works by Paula Rego, one of Portugal's leading contemporary artists, whose *Mãe* (1997) is outstanding. Pieces from major international artists such as David Hockney and Antony Gormley also feature.

PARQUE EDUARDO VII

MAP PP.100–101, POCKET MAP H4

The steep, formally laid out Parque Eduardo VII was named to honour Britain's King Edward VII when he visited the city in 1903. Its main building is the ornately tiled Pavilhão dos Desportos (Sports Pavilion), long ear-marked for much needed renovation. North of here is the main viewing platform which offers commanding vistas of the city as well as Ferris wheel during the summer months. Another highlight if you have children is the superb Parque Infantil (open daily; free), a play area built round a mock galleon.

Two huge, rambling **estufas** (daily: April–Sept 10am–7pm; Oct–March 9am–5pm; €3.10, free Sun until 2pm; Ⓦ www .estufafria.cm.lisboa.com) lie close by. Set in substantial former basalt quarries, both are filled with tropical plants, pools and endless varieties of palm and cactus. Of the two, the Estufa Quente (the hothouse) has the more exotic plants; the Estufa Fria (the coldhouse) hosts concerts and exhibitions.

Finally, the hilly northern reaches of the park contain an olive grove and a shallow lake which kids splash about in during the heat of the day.

PARQUE EDUARDO VII

CASA MUSEU DR ANASTÁCIO GONÇALVES

Avda 5 de Outubro 6–8. Entrance on Rua Pinheiro Chagas ☎ 213 540 823, Ⓦ www .cmag.imc-ip.pt. Tues 2–6pm, Wed–Sun 10am–6pm. €3. MAP PP.100–101, POCKET MAP J3.

This appealing neo-Romantic building with Art Nouveau touches – including a beautiful stained-glass window – was originally built for painter José Malhoa in 1904, but now holds the exquisite private collection of ophthalmologist Dr Anastácio Gonçalves, who bought the house in the 1930s. Highlights include paintings by Portuguese landscape artist João Vaz and by Malhoa himself, who specialized in historical paintings – his *Dream of Infante Henriques* is a typical example. You'll also find Chinese porcelain from the sixteenth-century Ming dynasty, along with furniture from England, France, Holland and Spain dating from the seventeenth century.

PRAÇA DE TOUROS

Campo Pequeno ☎ 217 998 450, Ⓦ www .campopequenotauromaquia.com. MAP PP.100–101, POCKET MAP J1.

Built in 1892, and substantially renovated in 2000 – with a retractable roof – the Praça de Touros at Campo Pequeno is an impressive Moorish-style bullring seating nine thousand spectators. The Portuguese *tourada* (bullfight) is not as famous as its Spanish counterpart, but as a spectacle it's marginally preferable, as here the bull isn't killed in the ring, but instead is wrestled to the ground in a genuinely elegant, colourful and skilled display. During the fight, however, the bull is usually injured and slaughtered later in any case. Performances start at around 10pm on Thursday evenings from Easter to September. At other times, you can visit a small museum which details the history of the arena which you can also visit as part of a tour (10am–1pm & 2–6pm, 7pm in summer; €5, arena visit only €3).

Surrounded by a ring of lively cafés and restaurants, the bullring also hosts concerts, live acts, musicals and other events. Beneath the arena is a surprisingly large underground shopping and cinema complex and a parking lot.

Ethnic Lisbon

In the fifteenth century hundreds of Africans came to Lisbon on slave ships during Portugal's ruthless maritime explorations. Today, over 120,000 people of African and Asian descent live in the Greater Lisbon area, most hailing originally from Portugal's former colonies – Cape Verde, Angola, Mozambique, Brazil, Goa and Macao. The 1974 revolution and subsequent independence of the former colonies saw another wave of immigrants settle in the capital. Nowadays African and Brazilian culture permeate Lisbon life, influencing its music, food, television and street slang. Most Lisboetas are rightly proud of their cosmopolitan city, although, inevitably, racism persists and few from ethnic minorities have managed to break through the glass ceiling to the top jobs.

JARDIM ZOOLÓGICO

Praça Marechal Humberto Delgado ☎ 217 232 900, ✆ www.zoolisboa.pt. Daily: March–Sept 10am–8pm; Oct–Feb 10am–6pm. €19.50, children under 12 €14. MAP PP.100–101, POCKET MAP E1

Lisbon's Jardim Zoológico was opened in 1884 and makes for an enjoyable excursion. There's a café-lined park area which you can visit for free and see monkeys, crocodiles and parrots. Once inside the zoo proper, a small cable car (daily from 11am until 30min before closing; included in the price) transports you over many of the animals, and there's a well-stocked reptile house and feeding sessions for sea lions and pelicans. Just by its main gates lies the Animax amusement park (daily 11am–7pm), where kids can load up a card for rides and games.

ESTÁDIO DA LUZ

☎ 707 200 100, ✆ www.slbenfica.pt. MAP PP.100–101

One of the most famous stadia in the world, the Estádio da Luz was built for and hosted the final of Euro 2004, when Portugal lost in a shock defeat to Greece. This is the home to Benfica (officially called Sport Lisboa e Benfica), the giant of Portuguese football who win (together with Porto) most domestic trophies. It's usually easy to buy match tickets from the stadium ticket office (from €23–50): expect to see the club mascot eagle flying across the pitch before the game starts. There is also an impressive museum (☎ 217 219 590; daily 10am–6pm, match days until kickoff; €10 or €15 with stadium tour) with interactive exhibits tracing the club's prestigious history, including its two European Cup wins (1961 and 1962) and recent Europa League finals in 2013 and 2014.

ESTÁDIO JOSÉ ALVALADE

Rua Professor Fernando da Fonseca, Apartado 4120 ☎ 217 516 000, ✆ www.sporting.pt. Ticket office open Mon–Fri 10am–8pm, and match days 10am–start of second half. MAP PP.100–101

The impressive José Alvalade Stadium is home to Sporting Clube de Portugal, better known as Sporting Lisbon. Seating over 50,000 spectators, the stadium was built for Euro 2004 adjacent to the original stadium. The team usually play second fiddle to city rivals Benfica (see above), but still boast an impressive array of trophies: over 18 league wins, 16 Portuguese Cup wins and a European Cup Winners Cup in 1964. Tickets for games (from €18–45) are available at the stadium ticket office. You can also visit the museum (Mon–Fri 11am–6pm; €10), which features the shirt of one of the club's best known sons, Cristiano Ronaldo.

Shops

AMOREIRAS

Avda Engenheiro Duarte Pacheco 2037. Bus #758 ⓦ www.amoreiras.com. Daily 10am–11pm. MAP PP.100-101, POCKET MAP F4

Amoreiras, Lisbon's striking, postmodern commercial centre, is a wild fantasy of pink and blue towers sheltering ten cinemas, sixty cafés and restaurants, 250 shops and a hotel. Built in 1985 and designed by adventurous Portuguese architect Tomás Taveira, most of its stores are open daily; Sunday sees the heaviest human traffic, with entire families descending for an afternoon out.

CENTRO COLOMBO

Avda Lusíada ⓜ Colégio Militar/Luz, ⓦ www.colombo.pt. Most shops daily 9am–midnight. MAP PP.100-101, POCKET MAP F1

Iberia's largest shopping centre is almost a town in its own right, with over 370 shops, 65 restaurants and ten cinema screens. Major stores include FNAC, Timberland, Sports Zone and Toys "R" Us, while the top floor has the usual fast-food outlets along with a sit-down dining area in the jungle-themed "Cidade Perdida" (Lost City).

EL CORTE INGLÉS

Avda António Augusto de Aguiar 31 ⓦ www.elcorteingles.pt. Most shops Mon–Sat 10am–10pm, Sun 10am–8pm. Cinema info on ☏ 707 232 221. MAP PP.100-101, POCKET MAP H3

A giant Spanish department store spread over nine floors, two of which are under-ground. The basement specializes in gourmet food, with various delis, bakers and a supermarket (closed Sun afternoon), while the upper

EL CORTE INGLÉS

floors offer a range of stylish goods, including clothes, sports gear, books, CDs and toys. The top floor packs in cafés and restaurants. There's also a fourteen-screen cinema in the basement.

MERCADO 31 DE JANEIRO

Rua Enginheiro Viera da Silva. Mon–Sat 7am–2pm. MAP PP.100-101, POCKET MAP J3

This bustling local market is divided into sections; you'll find a colourful array of fresh fruit, vegetables, spices, fish, flowers and a few crafts.

MISTURA DE ESTILOS

Rua São José 21. Mon–Fri 3–8pm (7pm in winter). MAP PP.100-101, POCKET MAP J5

This tiny shop sells individually crafted tiles from around €4 – as the name implies, the styles are mixed – from plain patterns to lovely animal motifs – but most are simple, effective and portable.

Restaurants

BENGAL TANDOORI

Rua da Alegria 23 ☎ 213 479 918, ⓦ www
.bengal.pt. Daily noon–midnight. MAP PP.100–101,
POCKET MAP J5

The decor might be Greco-Roman, but this is rated to be one of the best Indian restaurants in town, up a steep side-street. Expect all the usual dishes – madras, biryanis and of course excellent tandoori – in an intimate space with good service. Mains from €8–16.

CENTRO DE ARTE MODERNA

Rua Dr Bettencourt, Fundação Calouste
Gulbenkian ☎ 217 822 751. Mon & Wed–Sun
10am–5.45pm. MAP PP.96–97, POCKET MAP H2

Join the lunchtime queues at the museum restaurant for bargain hot and cold dishes. There's an excellent choice of salads for vegetarians. Similar food is offered in the basement of the Gulbenkian museum, with outdoor seats facing the gardens.

ELEVEN

Rua Marquês da Fronteira ☎ 213 862 211,
ⓦ www.restauranteleven.com. Mon–Sat
12.30–3pm & 7.30–11pm. MAP PP.100–101,
POCKET MAP G3

At the top of Parque Eduardo VII, this Michelin-starred

restaurant, under the watchful eye of German head chef Joachim Koerper, hits the heights both literally and metaphorically. The interior is both intimate and bright with wonderful city views. The food is expensive but not outrageous, with mains from around €30 or a tasting menu at €76. Dishes include sea bass with chestnuts, suckling pig with passion fruit or mixed fish with mushrooms, and there's a fine wine list.

GUILTY

Rua Barata Salgueiro 28 ☎ 211 913 590,
ⓦ www.guilty.olivier.pt. Tues–Sun 12.30–3.30pm
& 7.30pm–midnight, bar open Thurs–Sat until
4am. MAP PP.100–101, POCKET MAP H5

Classy comfort foods are served (hence the name) in this modern diner, including pasta, carpaccio, giant pizzas and gourmet burgers (mains €11–17) from renowned chef Olivier. Just off the Avenida da Liberdade, it's a fashionable spot, too, with nighttime DJs.

JARDIM DO SENTIDOS

Rua Mãe d'Água 3 ☎ 213 423 670. Mon–Fri
noon–3pm & 7–10.30pm, Sat 7–10.30pm.
MAP PP.100–101, POCKET MAP J5

This attractive, long space opens onto a pleasant garden. The food is vegetarian, with set buffet lunches (around €11) featuring the likes of *tofu á bras* and evening mains such as couscous and lasagne.

MARISQUEIRA SANTA MARTA

Trav do Enviato de Inglaterra 1 (off Rua de
Santa Marta) ☎ 213 525 638. Daily noon–
midnight. MAP PP.100–101, POCKET MAP J4

Attractive and spacious *marisqueira* with bubbling tanks of crabs in one corner. Service is very attentive and meals end with a complimentary port, after which you don't usually care that the bill is slightly above average (mains from €12).

ELEVEN

O CANTINHO DE SÃO JOSÉ

Rua São José 94 ☎ 213 427 866. Mon–Fri & Sun 11am–11pm. MAP PP.100–101, POCKET MAP J5

Friendly *tasca* serving good-value food – tuck into a full meal of grilled meat, salmon or other fish with wine and you may get change from €15.

RIBADOURO

Avda da Liberdade 155 ☎ 213 549 411, ⓦ www.cervejariaribadouro.pt. Daily noon–1am. MAP PP.100–101, POCKET MAP J5

The *avenida*'s best *cervejaria*, serving superb mixed grills (around €13), speciality prawns with garlic (around €15) and pricier shellfish (but no fish). If you don't fancy a full meal, take a seat at the bar and order a beer with a plate of prawns. It's best to book for the restaurant, especially at weekends.

A LINHA D'ÁGUA

Cafés

A LINHA D'ÁGUA

Jardim Amália Rodrigues ☎ 213 014 327. Daily 10am–midnight; Oct–March closes 8pm. MAP PP.100–101, POCKET MAP G3

Facing a small lake, this glass-fronted café is at the northern end of the park. It's a tranquil spot to sip a coffee or beer, and decent buffet lunches are served too.

GALETO

Avda da República 14 ☎ 213 560 269. Daily 7am–3am. MAP PP.100–101, POCKET MAP J2

Late-opening café with striking 1960s decor. and an array of snacks, pastries, beers and coffees. Drop in for a full meal at sensible prices by the bar.

PASTELARIA SANTA MARTA

Rua Rodrigues Sampaio 52 ☎ 213 533 901. Mon–Sat 7am–8pm. MAP PP.100–101, POCKET MAP J5

Unglamorous but popular local haunt with a superb array of cakes and snacks. A good spot

for inexpensive breakfasts and lunches. Pay at the till on exit.

VERSAILLES

Avda da República 15a ☎ 213 546 340. Daily 7.30am–10pm. MAP PP.100–101, POCKET MAP J2

This traditional café, full of bustling waiters, is busiest at around 4pm, when Lisbon's elderly dames gather for a chat beneath the chandeliers.

Bar

PANORAMA BAR

Sheraton Lisboa, Rua Latino Coelho 1 ☎ 213 120 000. Mon–Fri 1pm–2am, Sat 6pm–3am, Sun 6pm–2am. MAP PP.100–101, POCKET MAP J3.

Stroll into this high-rise hotel and take the lift to the spectacular top-floor cocktail bar (open to the public). Drinks aren't cheap, but dubbed Lisbon's eighth hill, the bar commands the best views of the city.

Music venue

HOT CLUBE DE PORTUGAL

Praça da Alegria 48 ☎ 213 460 305, ⓦ www .hcp.pt. Tues–Sat 10pm–2am. MAP PP.100–101, POCKET MAP J5

Dating from 1948 – making it one of Europe's oldest jazz clubs – this tiny basement club hosts top names in the jazz world, along with a range of local performers. The venue was largely rebuilt after a recent fire.

Parque das Nações

The Parque das Nações or "Park of Nations" (pronounced "na-soysh") is the high-tech former site of Expo '98. Its flat, pedestrianized walkways lined with fountains and futuristic buildings are in complete contrast to the narrow, precipitous streets of old Lisbon, and it is packed with locals on summer weekends. The main highlight is the giant Oceanário de Lisboa, but it also features a casino, a cable car, riverside walkways, a giant park and two of Lisbon's largest concert venues. It is also impossible to miss the astonishing 17km-long Vasco da Gama bridge over the Tejo. Constructed in time for the Expo in 1998, it is still the longest bridge in Europe.

OLIVAIS DOCK AND THE MEO ARENA

MAP P.111, POCKET MAP B17–18

The central focus of the Parque das Nações is the Olivais dock, overlooked by pixie-hatted twin towers, and where boats pull in on Tejo cruises (see p.146). The dock's **Marina** (ⓘ 218 949 066, ⓦ www.marinaparquedas nacoes.pt) offers canoeing and sailing lessons. The main building facing the dock is the Pavilhão de Portugal (Portugal Pavilion), a multipurpose arena designed by Álvaro Siza Vieira, architect of the reconstructed Chiado district, featuring an enormous, sagging concrete canopy on its south side. It now hosts temporary exhibitions. Opposite here – past Antony Gormley's weird *Rhizone* sculpture, a tree of cast-iron legs – is the spaceship-like **MEO Arena** (ⓘ 218 918 440, ⓦ www.arena.meo.pt), Portugal's largest indoor arena and the venue for major visiting bands (including One Direction, Justin Bieber, Coldplay and Madonna) and sporting events. It also hosted the 2005 MTV Europe Music Awards.

Visiting the park

The best way to reach the park is to take the metro to Oriente or bus #728 from Praça do Comércio. Oriente metro station exits in the bowels of the Estação do Oriente, a cavernous glass and concrete station designed by Spanish architect Santiago Calatrava.

The park's website (ⓘ 218 919 333, ⓦ www.portaldasnacoes.pt) has details of the day's events, and details of the urban art dotted round the area, from murals and graffiti art to statues and sculptures.

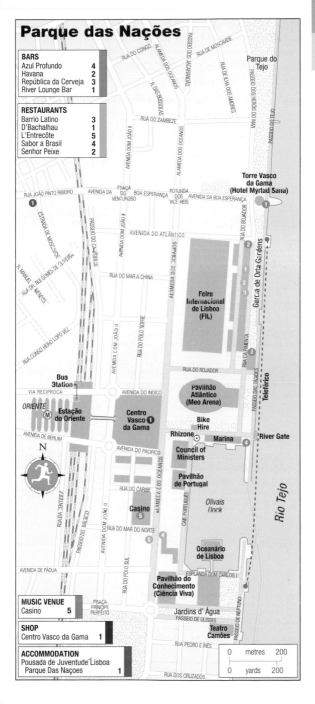

Parque das Nações

BARS

Azul Profundo	4
Havana	2
República da Cerveja	3
River Lounge Bar	1

RESTAURANTS

Barrio Latino	3
D'Bachalhau	1
L'Entrecôte	5
Sabor a Brasil	4
Senhor Peixe	2

MUSIC VENUE

Casino	5

SHOP

Centro Vasco da Gama	1

ACCOMMODATION

Pousada de Juventude Lisboa Parque Das Nações	1

PAVILHÃO DO CONHECIMENTO (CIÊNCIA VIVA)

Alameda dos Oceanos ☎ 218 917 100,
ⓦ www.pavconhecimento.pt. Tues–Fri
10am–6pm, Sat & Sun 11am–7pm. €8,
children under 17 €5. MAP P.111, POCKET MAP B18

Run by Portugal's Ministry of
Science and Technology, the
Knowledge Pavilion (Live
Science) hosts excellent
changing exhibitions on
subjects like 3D animation
and the latest computer
technology, and is usually
bustling with school parties.
The permanent interactive
exhibits – allowing you to
create a vortex in water or a
film of detergent the size of a
baby's blanket – are particularly
good and there's also a
cybercafé offering free internet.

JARDINS DA ÁGUA

MAP P.111, POCKET MAP B19

The Jardins da Água (Water
Gardens), crisscrossed by
waterways and ponds, are
based on the stages of a river's
drainage pattern, from stream
to estuary. They are not huge,
but linked by stepping stones,
and there are enough gushing

fountains, water gadgets and
pumps to keep children
occupied for hours.

OCEANÁRIO

Esplanada Dom Carlos I ☎ 218 917 002,
ⓦ www.oceanario.pt. Daily: May–Sept
10am–8pm; Oct–April 10am–6pm. €14,
children under 12 €11, family ticket €36.
MAP P.111, POCKET MAP B18

Designed by Peter Chermaeff
and looking like something off
the set of a James Bond film,
Lisbon's Oceanário
(Oceanarium) is one of
Europe's largest and contains
some 8000 fish and marine
animals. Its main feature is the
enormous central tank which
you can look into from
different levels for close-up
views of circling sharks down
to the rays burying themselves
in the sand. Almost more
impressive, though, are the
re-creations of various ocean
ecosystems, such as the
Antarctic tank, containing
frolicking penguins, and the
Pacific tank, where otters bob
about in the rock pools. On a
darkened lower level, smaller
tanks contain shoals of brightly
coloured tropical fish and other
warm-water creatures. Find a
window free of school parties
and the whole experience
becomes the closest you'll get
to deep-sea diving without
getting wet.

THE TELEFÉRICO AND THE JARDINS GARCIA DA ORTA

ⓦ www.telecabinelisboa.pt. Daily: May to
mid-Sept 10.30am–8pm; mid-Sept–Oct &
mid-March–April 11am–7pm; Nov–mid-March
11am–6pm. €4 one-way, €6 return. Children
under 12 €2 single, €3.50 return. MAP P.111,
POCKET MAP B16–18

The ski-lift-style *teleférico*
(cable car) rises up to 20m as it
shuttles you over Olivais Docks
to the northern side of the
Parque, giving commanding

JARDINS DA ÁGUA

views over the site on the way. It drops down to the Garcia da Orta gardens, containing exotic trees from Portugal's former colonies. Behind the gardens, Rua Pimenta is lined with a motley collection of international restaurants, from Irish to Israeli.

TORRE VASCO DA GAMA

Cais das Naus ☎ 211 107 600, Ⓦ www.myriad.pt. MAP P.111, POCKET MAP B16

Once an integral part of an oil refinery, the Torre Vasco da Gama (Vasco da Gama Tower) is, at 145m high, Lisbon's tallest structure. The tower is now integrated into the five-star hotel *Myriad Sana*, Lisbon's answer to Dubai's *Burj Al Arab*.

PARQUE DO TEJO

MAP P.111, POCKET MAP B15

Spreading along the waterfront for 2km right up to the Vasco da Gama bridge, Parque do Tejo is Lisbon's newest park, with bike trails and riverside walks. It's a great spot for a picnic – supplies are available in the Vasco da Gama shopping centre.

FEIRA INTERNACIONAL DE LISBOA

Rua do Bojador ☎ 218 921 500, Ⓦ www.fil.pt. MAP P.111, POCKET MAP B16–17

Lisbon's trade fair hall, the Feira Internacional de Lisboa (FIL), hosts various events, including a handicrafts fair displaying ceramics and crafts from around the country (usually in July).

Vasco da Gama

The opening of Parque das Nações in 1998 celebrated the 500th anniversary of Vasco da Gama's arrival in India. One of Portugal's greatest explorers, Da Gama was born in Sines in 1460. By the 1490s he was working for João II protecting trading stations along the African coast. This persuaded the next king, Manuel I, to commission him to find a sea route to India. He departed Lisbon in July 1497 with a fleet of four ships, reaching southern Africa in December. The following May they finally reached Calicut in southwest India, obtaining trading terms before departing in August 1498. The return voyage took a full year, by which time Da Gama had lost two of his ships and half his men. But he was richly rewarded by the king, his voyage inspiring Camões to write *Os Lusíadas*, Portugal's most famous epic poem. Da Gama returned to India twice more, the final time in 1524 when he contracted malaria and died in the town of Cochin.

CENTRO VASCO DA GAMA

Shops

CENTRO VASCO DA GAMA

Avda D. João II 40 ☎ 218 930 600, Ⓦ www
.centrovascodagama.pt. Daily 9am–midnight.
MAP P.111, POCKET MAP B17

Three floors of local and
international stores are housed
under a glass roof, washed by
permanently running water;
international branches include
Zara, Timberland, Swatch and
C&A, and local sports and
bookshops also feature. There
are plenty of fast-food outlets
and good-value restaurants on
the top floor, ten cinema screens,
children's areas and a Continente
supermarket on the lower floor.

Restaurants

BARRIO LATINO

Rua de Pimenta 31 ☎ 934 971 585,
Ⓦ www.barriolatinolisboa.com. Daily
noon–4am. MAP P.111, POCKET MAP B16

A decent bar and restaurant
(steak and fish from around
€12) but best known for its

riotous Afro-Latin *kizomba*
dance nights. Pop in for some
dance lessons (Wed–Sun 11pm
onwards), or just come along
and join in the fun.

D'BACALHAU

Rua do Pimenta 43–45 ☎ 218 941 296,
Ⓦ www.restaurantebacalhau.com. Daily
noon–4pm & 7–11pm. MAP P.111, POCKET MAP B16

If you want to sample one of
the alleged 365 recipes for
bacalhau – salted cod – this is
a good place to come, as it
serves quite a range of them
from €9: *bacalhau com natas*
(with a creamy sauce) is
always good. There are also
other dishes, including a
selection of fresh fish and
meat dishes from €11.

L'ENTRECÔTE

Alameda dos Oceanos 1.02.12a ☎ 218 962
220. Daily 12.30–3pm & 7.30–11.30pm.
MAP P.111, POCKET MAP B18

Local branch of the Lisbon
restaurant famed for its
fabulous steaks cooked with
sublime sauces – choose from
various menus starting at €10.

SABOR A BRASIL

Alameda dos Oceanos, Edifício Lisboa 1990
☎ 218 955 143, Ⓦ www.saborabrasil.com.
Daily noon–3.30am & 7.30–11.30pm. MAP P.111,
POCKET MAP B18

This large space has outdoor
seats in a great position facing
the waters. Its name means
"taste of Brazil" and you can
sample a range of piquant
dishes such as spicy *moqueca*
fish, tropical salmon, *feijoada*
bean stews or *picanha* garlic
beef from €12–15. Live music
at weekends.

SENHOR PEIXE

Rua da Pimenta 35–37 ☎ 218 955 892.
Tues–Sat noon–3.30pm & 7–10.30pm, Sun
noon–3.30pm. MAP P.111, POCKET MAP B16

"Mr Fish" is widely thought to
serve up some of the best

fresh seafood in the Lisbon region – check the counter for the day's catch or choose a lobster from the bubbling tank. Most dishes – from around €15 – are grilled in the open kitchen. There's also a little fish-themed bar and pleasant outdoor tables.

Bars

AZUL PROFUNDO

Rossio dos Olivais, Quiosque 4. Daily 10am–2am, closes 10pm from Oct–April. MAP P.111, POCKET MAP B17

Sunny esplanade bar overlooking the glittering docks. Offers a good range of snacks, fruit juices and fantastic *caipirinha* cocktails along with inexpensive lunches.

HAVANA

Rua da Pimenta 115–117. Tues–Thurs & Sun noon–2am, Fri & Sat noon–4am. MAP P.111, POCKET MAP B16

Lively Cuban bar with an airy interior and outdoor seating. The pulsating Latin sounds get

progressively louder after 11pm, when it turns into more of a club. You can also take dance lessons on Thursdays and Fridays.

REPÚBLICA DA CERVEJA

Jardim das Tágides 2.26.01 ☎ 218 922 590. Mon–Sat 12.30pm–1am, closes midnight from Oct–Feb. MAP P.111, POCKET MAP B17

In a great position close to the water's edge and facing the Vasco da Gama bridge, this modern bar-restaurant specializes in some fine international beers, though sticking to the local Super bock will save a few euros. Steaks, burgers and sausages are also on offer (mains from €10–16), and there's occasional live music.

RIVER LOUNGE BAR

Myriad Sana Hotel, Cais das Nouc, Lote 2.23.01 ☎ 211 107 600, ✆ www.myriad.pt. Daily noon–midnight. MAP P.111, POCKET MAP B16

Inside the deluxe *Myriad Sana Hotel*, this ultrahip *River Lounge Bar* juts into the Tejo so you feel as if you're right on the water. Cocktails and drinks are predictably expensive, but it's worth it for the view. Frequent live music after 7pm.

Music venue

CASINO

Alameda dos Oceanos 1.03.01 ☎ 218 929 000, ✆ www.casinolisboa.pt. Sun–Thurs 3pm–3am, Fri–Sat 4pm–4am. MAP P.111, POCKET MAP A18

Opened in 2006, this state-of-the-art space – with its glass-cylinder entrance hall – hosts top shows from Broadway and London as well as major concerts in the performance hall, which has a retractable roof. The usual casino attractions also feature.

COFFEE AND PASTEL DE NATA

Sintra

If you make just one day-trip from Lisbon, choose the beautiful hilltop town of Sintra, the former summer residence of Portuguese royalty and a UNESCO World Heritage Site since 1995. Not only does the town boast two of Portugal's most extraordinary palaces, it also contains a semitropical garden, a Moorish castle, a top modern-art museum and proximity to some great beaches. Looping around a series of wooded ravines and with a climate that encourages moss and ferns to grow from every nook and cranny, Sintra consists of three districts: Sintra-Vila, with most of the historical attractions; Estefânia, a ten-minute walk to the east, where trains from Lisbon pull in; and São Pedro to the south, well known for its antique shops and best visited on the eve of São Pedro (June 28–29), the main saint's day, and for its market on the second and fourth Sunday of the month.

SINTRA-VILA

The historic centre of Sintra spreads across the slopes of several steep hills, themselves loomed over by wooded heights topped by the Moorish castle and the Palácio da Pena. Dominating the centre of Sintra-Vila are the tapering chimneys of the Palácio Nacional, surrounded by an array of tall houses painted in pale pink, ochre or mellow yellow, many with ornate turrets and decorative balconies peering out to the plains of Lisbon far below. All this is highly scenic – though in fact Sintra looks at its best seen on the way in from the station. Summer crowds can swamp the narrow central streets, and once you've seen the sights, you're best off heading to the surrounding attractions up in the hills.

Visiting Sintra

There are trains from Lisbon's Rossio station (every 20–60min; 45min; €2.65 single). A land train (every 30min from 10.30am–dusk; €5 day-ticket) runs from Sintra station to São Pedro and back via Sintra-Vila. Alternatively, bus #434 takes a circular route from Sintra station to most of the sites mentioned in this chapter (every 20–40min from 9.45am–6.15pm; €5) and allows you to get on and off whenever you like on the circuit. Also useful is bus #435 which runs from Sintra station to Monserrate gardens via Sintra-Vila and Quinta da Regaleira (every 45min 9.45am–6.15pm; €3 return) To see the area around Sintra, including the coast, consider a Day-rover (Turístico Diário) ticket on the local Scotturb buses (ⓦ www.scotturb.com; €12). Ask at the tourist office about various combined tickets that can save money on entry to the main sites.

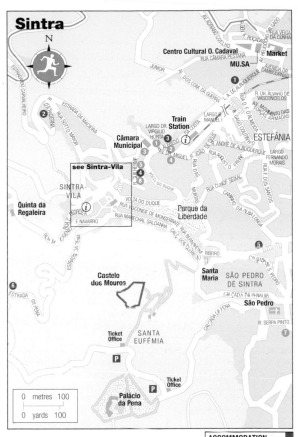

Sintra

N

Centro Cultural O. Cadaval
RUA CÂMARA PESTANA
MU.SA ❶
Market

JUNIOR
AV. DOS COM. DA GUERRA

AVENIDA DR. CAMBOURNAC

R. DR. ÁLVARO DE VASCONCELOS

R. DA ENG

AV. MOVIMENTO DAS FORÇAS ARMADAS

ESTRADA DA MADEIRA

D'ALPOCERNA ❷

RUA DA SOTTO MAYOR

Train
Station ❶
LARGO DR. VIRGILIO HORTA ❸
Câmara Municipal ❸
AV. ALFREDO
CALÇ DA MIGUEL R. JOÃO DE DEUS
RUA DAS MURTINS
VOLTA DO DUQUE

LARGO MANUEL I

R. GAGO DOUTINHA
R. ANDRÉ DE ALBUQUERQUE

ESTEFÂNIA

LARGO FERNANDO MORAIS
RUA AUGUSTO FERRE
RUA F. DOS SANTOS

see Sintra-Vila

SINTRA-VILA ⓘ

Quinta da Regaleira

F. NAVARRO
RUA VISCONDE DE MONSERRATE RUA BERENIM
RUA MARECHAL SALDANHA CALÇ DOS CLERICOS

Parque da Liberdade

RUA COND SEXUAL

CAMINHO DA ALBA LONGA

RIBEIRO ❺

ESTRADA DE PENA ❻

Castelo dos Mouros

Santa Maria

SÃO PEDRO DE SINTRA

CALÇADA DA PENA NOVA

São Pedro

R. SERPA PINTO ❼

Ticket Office

SANTA EUFÉMIA

🅿

Ticket Office 🅿

Palácio da Pena

0 metres 100
0 yards 100

Sintra-Vila

Palácio Nacional

RUA SOTTO MAYOR
RUA PASSEIO DOS VELHOS
RUA CONS SEGRADO

CALÇADA DOS FERRO DO PORTO

LARGO RAINHA D. AMÉLIA ❶

RUA DA PENDOA

✉

❽

PRAÇA DA REPÚBLICA ⓘ
❿

RUA FRESCA

VOLTA DO DUQUE

RUA GIL VICENTE

RUA VISCONDE DE MONSERRATE

N

RUA CONSIGLIERI PEDROSO

RUA FONTE DA PIPA

LARGO FERREIRA DE CASTRO

❷

⓫ RUA A. EUGENIA F. NAVARRO

ACCOMMODATION
Casa do Valle	2
Chalet Relogio	6
Chalet Saudade	3
Hotel Nova Sintra	1
Hotel Sintra Jardim	5
Moon Hill Hostel	4

RESTAURANTS
A Tasca do Manel	3
Caldo Entornado	6
Cantinho de São Pedro	7
Incomum	2
Páteo do Garrett	11
Restaurante Regional	1
Tulhas	10

CAFÉS
Adega das Caves	8
Casa Piriquita	9
Fábrica das Verdadeiras Queijadas da Sapa	5
Saudade	4

BARS
Bar Fonte da Pipa	2
Café Paris	1

PALÁCIO NACIONAL

Largo da Rainha Dona Amélia ☎ 219 106 840. ⊛ www.pnsintra.imc-ip.pt. Daily: March–Oct 9.30am–7pm; Nov–Feb 9.30am–5.30pm. €10. MAP P.117

Best seen early or late in the day to avoid the crowds, the sumptuous Palácio Nacional was probably already in existence at the time of the Moors. It takes its present form from the rebuilding of Dom João I (1385–1433) and his successor, Dom Manuel I, the chief royal beneficiary of Vasco da Gama's explorations. Its exterior style is an amalgam of Gothic – featuring impressive battlements – and Manueline, tempered inside by a good deal of Moorish influence. Sadly, after the fall of the monarchy in 1910, most of the surrounding walls and medieval houses were destroyed. Highlights on the lower floor include the Manueline **Sala dos Cisnes**, so-called for the swans (*cisnes*) on its ceiling, and the Sala das Pegas, which takes its name from the flock of magpies (*pegas*) painted on the frieze and ceiling – João I, caught in the act of kissing a lady-in-waiting by his queen, reputedly had the room decorated with as many magpies as there were women at court, to imply they were all magpie-like gossips.

Best of the upper floor is the gallery above the palace chapel. Beyond, a succession of **state rooms** finishes with the Sala das Brasões, its domed and coffered ceiling emblazoned with the arms of 72 noble families. Finally, don't miss the kitchens, whose roofs taper into the giant chimneys that are the palace's distinguishing features. The Palace also hosts events for the Sintra Music Festival (see p.150).

MU.SA

Avda Heliodoro Salgado ☎ 965 233 692, ⊛ www.cm-sintra.pt. Tues–Sun 10am–6pm. Free. MAP P.117

Inside Sintra's beautiful former casino, this appealing contemporary art museum is dedicated to important contemporary Portuguese artists such as Eílio de Paula Campos (1184–1943), who portrays traditional rural scenes, and innovative sculptress Dorita Castel-Branco (1936–1996). There is also a photography room and temporary exhibits.

QUINTA DA REGALEIRA

Rua Barbosa do Bocage. Daily: Feb, March & Oct 10am–6.30pm; April–Sept 10am–8pm; Nov–Jan 10am–5.30pm. Tours (90min) every 30–60min; advance booking essential on ☎ 219 106 650, ⓦ www.regaleira.pt. €10. Unguided visits €6. MAP P.117

The Quinta da Regaleira is one of Sintra's most elaborate estates. It was designed at the end of the nineteenth century by Italian architect and theatre set designer Luigi Manini for wealthy Brazilian merchant António Augusto Carvalho Monteiro. Manini's penchant for the dramatic is obvious: the principal building, the mock-Manueline Palácio dos Milhões, sprouts turrets and towers, while the interior boasts Art Nouveau tiles and elaborate Rococo wooden ceilings

The surrounding **gardens** shelter fountains, terraces and grottoes, with the highlight being the Initiation Well, inspired by the initiation practices of the Freemasons. Entering via a Harry Potter-esque revolving stone door, you walk down a moss-covered spiral staircase to the foot of the well and through a tunnel, which eventually resurfaces at the edge of a lake (though in winter you exit from a shorter tunnel so as not to disturb a colony of hibernating bats).

In summer, the gardens host occasional performances of live music, usually classical or jazz.

CASTELO DOS MOUROS

☎ 219 237 300, ⓦ www.parquedesintra.pt. Daily: March–Oct 9.30am–8pm; Nov–Feb 10am–6pm. €8. MAP P.117

Reached on bus #434, or a steep drive, the ruined ramparts of the Castelo dos Mouros are truly spectacular.

It's also a pleasant, if steep, walk up (30–40min): start at the Calçada dos Clérigos, near the church of Santa Maria, where a stone pathway leads all the way up to the lower slopes, where you can see a Moorish grain silo and a ruined twelfth-century church. To enter the castle itself, you'll need to buy a ticket from the road exit. Built in the ninth century, the castle was taken from the Moors in 1147 by Afonso Henriques, Portugal's first monarch: the ruins of a Moorish mosque remain. The castle walls were allowed to fall into disrepair over subsequent centuries, though they were restored in the mid-nineteenth century under the orders of Ferdinand II. The castle is partly built into two craggy pinnacles, and views from up here are dazzling both inland and across to the Atlantic. Recent excavations have revealed the ruins of Muslim houses, thirty medieval Christian graves and ceramic vases dating back to the fiffth century BC.

CASTELO DOS MOUROS

PALÁCIO DA PENA

Estrada da Pena ☎ 219 237 300, ⊛ www
.parquedesintra.pt. Daily: March–Oct
9.45am–7pm; Nov–Feb 10am–6pm; last entry
1hr before closing. Palace and gardens €14,
gardens only €7.50; reduced prices from
Nov–Feb. MAP P.117

Bus #434 stops opposite the
lower entrance to Parque da
Pena, a stretch of rambling
woodland with a scattering of
lakes and follies. At the top of
the park, about twenty minutes'
walk from the entrance or a
short ride on a shuttle bus (€3
return), looms the fabulous
Palácio da Pena, a wild fantasy
of domes, towers, ramparts and
walkways, approached through
mock-Manueline gateways and
a drawbridge that does not
draw. A compelling riot of
kitsch, the palace was built in
the 1840s to the specifications
of Ferdinand of Saxe-Coburg-

Gotha, husband of Queen
Maria II, with the help of the
German architect, Baron
Eschwege. The interior is
preserved exactly as it was left
by the royal family when they
fled Portugal in 1910. The
result is fascinating: rooms of
stone decorated to look like
wood, statues of turbaned
Moors nonchalantly holding
electric chandeliers – it's all
here. Of an original convent,
founded in the early sixteenth
century to celebrate the first
sight of Vasco da Gama's
returning fleet, only a
beautiful, tiled chapel and
Manueline cloister have
been retained.

You can also look round the
mock-Alpine **Chalet Condessa
d'Edla** (€9.50, includes entry
to park), built by Ferdinand in
the 1860s as a retreat for his
second wife.

MONSERRATE

Estrada da Monserrate ☎ 219 237 300.
ⓦ www.parquedesintra.pt Daily: March–Oct
9.30am–7pm; Nov–Feb 10am–5pm. €8.
MAP BELOW

The name most associated with
the fabulous gardens and
palace of Monserrate is that of
William Beckford, the
wealthiest untitled Englishman
of his age, who rented the
estate from 1793 to 1799,
having been forced to flee
Britain after he was caught in
a compromising position with
a sixteen-year-old boy. Setting
about improving the place, he
landscaped a waterfall and even
imported a flock of sheep from
his estate.

Half a century later, a second
immensely rich Englishman,
Sir Francis Cook, bought the
estate and imported the head
gardener from Kew to lay out
water plants, tropical ferns and

palms, and just about every
known conifer. For a time
Monserrate boasted the only
lawn in Iberia, and it remains
one of Europe's most richly
stocked gardens, with over a
thousand different species of
subtropical tree and plant.

From the entrance, paths lead
steeply down through lush
undergrowth to a ruined
chapel, half engulfed by a giant
banyan tree. From here, lawns
take you up to Cook's main
legacy, a great **Victorian palace**
inspired by Brighton Pavilion,
with its mix of Moorish and
Italian decoration – the dome
is modelled on the Duomo in
Florence. The interior has been
restored after years of neglect,
and you can now admire the
amazingly intricate plasterwork
which covers almost every wall
and ceiling. The park also has a
decent café (daily 10am–6pm).

AZENHAS DO MAR

Bus #441 from Sintra (every 1–2hr; 40min).
MAP P.121

Whitewashed cottages tumble down the steep cliff-face at the pretty village of Azenhas do Mar, one of the most lively villages of the Sintra coast. The beach is small, but there are artificial seawater pools for swimming in when the ocean is too rough.

PRAIA DAS MAÇÃS

Bus #441 from Sintra (every 1–2hr; 30min); or Praia das Maçãs tram from Sintra (see box opposite). MAP P.121

The largest and liveliest resort on this coast, Praia das Maçãs is also the easiest to reach from Sintra – take the tram (see box below) for the most enjoyable journey. Along with a big swath of sand, Praia das Maçãs has an array of bars and restaurants to suit all budgets.

PRAIA GRANDE

Bus #441 from Sintra (every 1–2hr; 25min).
MAP P.121

Set in a wide, sandy cliff-backed bay, this is one of the best and safest beaches on the Sintra coast, though its breakers attract surfers aplenty. In August the World Bodyboarding Championships are held here,

along with games such as volleyball and beach rugby. Plenty of inexpensive cafés and restaurants are spread out along the beachside road, and if the sea gets too rough, there are giant sea pools on the approach to the beach (June–Sept; €10).

PRAIA DA ADRAGA

No public transport; by car, follow the signs from the village of Almoçageme. POCKET MAP P.121

Praia da Adraga was flatteringly voted one of Europe's best beaches by a British newspaper; the unspoilt, cliff-backed, sandy bay with just one beach restaurant is certainly far quieter than the other resorts, but it takes the full brunt of the Atlantic, so you'll need to take great care when swimming.

Quaint old trams shuttle from near the Centro Cultural Olga Cadaval to the coastal resort of Praia das Maçãs via Colares (April–June & Sept Fri–Sun three daily, July & Aug Wed & Thurs three daily, Fri–Sun six daily; 50min; €3 single). However, check the latest routes and timetables on ☎219 236 920 or in the Sintra tourist office, as there are frequent shortenings of the route or alterations to the service.

CABO DA ROCA

Bus #403 from Sintra or Cascais train stations (every 90min; 45min). MAP P.121

Little more than a windswept rocky cape with a lighthouse, this is the most westerly point in mainland Europe, which guarantees a steady stream of visitors – get there early to avoid the coach parties. You can soak up the views from the café-restaurant and handicraft shop (daily 9.30am–7.30pm) and buy a certificate to prove you've been here at the little tourist office (daily 9am–8pm, closes 7pm from Oct–May; ☎ 219 280 081).

CONVENTO DOS CAPUCHOS

No public transport. A return taxi from Sintra with a 1hr stopover costs around €40 ☎ 219 237 381, ⊕ www.parquesdesintra.pt. Daily: March–Oct 9.30am–8pm; Nov–Feb 10am–6pm. €7. MAP P.121

If you have your own transport, don't miss a trip to the Convento dos Capuchos, an extraordinary hermitage with tiny, dwarf-like cells cut from the rock and lined with cork – hence its popular name of the Cork Convent. It was occupied for three hundred years until being finally abandoned in 1834 by its seven

remaining monks, who must have found the gloomy warren of rooms and corridors too much to maintain. Some rooms – the penitents' cells – can only be entered by crawling through 70cm-high doors; here, and on every other ceiling, doorframe and lintel, are attached panels of cork, taken from the surrounding woods. Elsewhere, you'll come across a washroom, kitchen, refectory, tiny chapels, and even a bread oven set apart from the main complex.

PENINHA

MAP P.121

With your own transport, it is worth exploring the dramatic wooded landscape between Capuchos and Coba da Roca, much of it studded with giant moss-covered boulders. Some 3km from Capuchos lies Peninha, a spectacularly sited hermitage perched on a granite crag. The sixteenth-century Baroque interior is usually locked, but climb up anyway to get dazzling views of the Sintra coast towards Cascais. You can also take a waymarked 4.5km trail round the crag; otherwise it is a short return walk from the woodland car park.

CONVENTO DOS CAPUCHOS

Restaurants

A TASCA DO MANEL

Largo Dr. Virgílio Horta 5 ☎ 219 230 215. Mon–Fri 7.30am–8pm, Sat 7.30am–7pm. MAP P.117

In total contrast to Sintra's wonderfully ornate Town Hall opposite, this is a simple but recommended little *tasca* with cured hams hanging over the bar. Squeeze into a table for very good value, no-nonsense fish, stews and grills from around €7.

CALDO ENTORNADO

Rua Guilherme Gomes Fernandes 19 ☎ 219 244 149, Ⓦ www.caldo-entornado.pt. Daily 12.30–3pm & 7–10.30pm. MAP P.117

Attached to the *Moon Hill* hostel (see p.141), this cosy, good-value contemporary restaurant serves creative Portuguese dishes – try the tasty stuffed squid with coriander rice (€11), or loin of boar (€14).

CANTINHO DE SÃO PEDRO

Praça D. Fernando II 18, São Pedro de Sintra ☎ 219 230 267, Ⓦ www.cantinhosaopedro.com. Daily noon–3pm & 7.30–10pm. MAP P.117

Large restaurant with bare stone walls overlooking an attractive courtyard just off São Pedro's main square. The traditional dishes (such as *bacalhau com natas*) are better than the international ones. Mains from €9. On cool evenings a log fire keeps things cosy.

INCOMUM

Rua Dr. Alfredo Costa 22, Sintra ☎ 219 243 719, Ⓦ www.incomumbyluissantos.pt. Mon, Wed–Fri & Sun noon–midnight, Sat 4.30pm–midnight. MAP P.117

Close to the station, this upmarket restaurant and wine bar is run by chef Luís Santos. His stints in some of Switzerland's top restaurants are reflected in a menu featuring the likes of scallops with mushroom risotto, black linguini with seafood and steak with sweet potatoes, though the ingredients are local and top quality. Mains from €15.

PÁTEO DO GARRETT

Rua Maria Eugénia Reis F. Navarro 7 ☎ 219 243 380, Ⓦ www.pateodogarrett.com. Mon, Tues & Thurs–Sun 11am–11pm; Jan–April 11am–2pm. MAP P.117

Although this café-restaurant has a dark, dim interior, it's also got a lovely sunny patio offering fine views over the village. Serves mixed meat kebabs, monkfish rice and the like from around €12–14, or just pop in for a drink.

RESTAURANTE REGIONAL DE SINTRA

Trav do Município 1 ☎ 219 234 444. Mon, Tues & Thurs–Sun noon–4pm & 7–10.30pm. MAP P.117

In a lovely old building next to the Câmara Municipal, this traditional and slightly formal restaurant serves tasty dishes at

QUEIJADAS DA SINTRA

CAFÉ PARIS

queueing to buy *queijadas da Sintra* (sweet cheesecakes) and other pastries.

FÁBRICA DAS VERDADEIRAS QUEIJADAS DA SAPA

Volta do Duche 12 ☎ 219 230 493. Tues–Fri 9am–7pm, Sat & Sun 9am–8pm. MAP P.117

This old-fashioned café is famed for its traditional *queijadas*, made on the premises for over a century. It's a bit dingy inside, so it's best to buy takeaways to sustain you on your walk to the centre.

SAUDADE

Avda Dr. Miguel Bombarda 6, Sintra ☎ 212 428 804, Ⓦ www.saudade.pt. Daily 0.30am–8pm. MAP P.117

This buzzy café used to be a factory selling *queijadas* and has a warren of rooms and its own art gallery, with occasional live music. As well as cakes, scones and sandwiches, it serves some interesting *petiscos* such as Madeiran garlic bread and regional cheeses. A wide range of drinks and teas include Gorreana tea from the Azores.

reasonable prices – fresh fish from €12, grilled meats from €10–15 and a very good *crepe de marisco* (seafood crêpe) for €10.

TULHAS

Rua Gil Vicente 4–6 ☎ 219 232 378 Mon, Tues & Thurs–Sun noon–3.30pm & 7–10pm. MAP P.117

Imaginative cooking in a fine building converted from old grain silos – the old grain well takes pride of place in the floor. The giant mixed grills at €25 for two will keep carnivores happy, while the weekend specials are usually good value with meat and fish from around €10.

Cafés

ADEGA DAS CAVES

Rua da Pendoa 2–10 ☎ 219 239 848, Ⓦ www .adegadascaves.com. Daily 10am–2am. MAP P.117

Bustling café-bar in the former palace coal merchant's, attracting a predominantly local and youthful clientele; the restaurant does meals from around €9.

CASA PIRIQUITA

Rua das Padarias 1 ☎ 219 230 626. Mon, Tues & Thurs–Sun 9am–9pm. MAP P.117

Cosy tearoom and bakery, which can get busy with locals

Bars

BAR FONTE DA PIPA

Rua Fonte da Pipa 11–13 ☎ 219 234 437. Daily 9pm–3am. MAP P.117

Laidback bar with low lighting, comfy chairs and a fine sangria. It's up the hill from *Casa Piriquita*, next to the lovely ornate fountain (*fonte*) that the street is named after.

CAFÉ PARIS

Praçe da República 32 ☎ 219 232 375. Daily 9am–midnight. MAP P.117

This attractive blue-tiled café-bar is the highest-profile in town, which means steep prices for not especially exciting food, although it is a great place for a cocktail.

The Lisbon coast

Lisbon's most accessible beaches lie along the Cascais coast just beyond the point where the Tejo flows into the Atlantic. Famed for its casino, Estoril has the best sands, though neighbouring Cascais has more buzz. The River Tejo separates Lisbon from high-rise Caparica, to the south, on a superb stretch of wave-pounded beach, popular with surfers.

ESTORIL

With its grandiose villas, luxury hotels and health spa, Estoril (pronounced é-stril) has pretensions towards being a Portuguese Riviera. The centre is focused on the leafy **Parque do Estoril** and its enormous casino (daily 3pm–3am; free; semiformal attire required; ☎214 667 700, ⓦ www.casino -estoril.pt). During World War II, this was where exiled

royalty hung out and many spies made their names. Ian Fleming was based here to keep an eye on double agents, and used his experience at the casino as inspiration for the first James Bond novel, *Casino Royale*.

The resort's fine sandy beach, **Praia de Tamariz**, is backed by some ornate villas and a seafront promenade that stretches northwest to Cascais, a pleasant twenty-minute stroll.

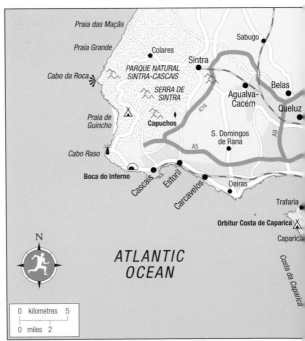

In summer, firework displays take place above the beach every Saturday at midnight.

Estoril is also famed for its world-class **golf courses** which lie a short distance inland (info at Ⓦ www.portugalgolf.pt); it also hosts the Estoril Open tennis tournament in May (Ⓦ www.millenniumestoril open.com).

Transport to Estoril and Cascais

Trains from Lisbon's Cais do Sodré (every 15–20min; 35min to Estoril, 40min to Cascais; €2.65 single) wend along the shore. There are also regular buses to and from Sintra, or it's a fine drive down the corniche.

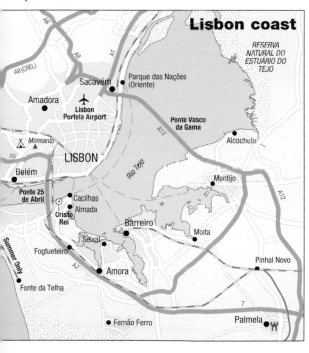

CASCAIS

MAP BELOW

Cascais (pronounced cash-kaysh) is a highly attractive former fishing village, liveliest round Largo Luís de Camões, at one end of Rua Frederico Arouca, the main mosaic-paved pedestrian thoroughfare.

Praia da Conceição is ideal to lounge on or try out watersports. The rock-fringed smaller beaches of **Praia da Rainha** and **Praia da Ribeira** are off the central stretch, while regular buses run 6km northwest to **Praia do Guincho**, a fabulous sweep of surf-beaten sands.

Cascais is at its most charming in the grid of streets north of the **Igreja da Assunção** – its *azulejos* predate the earthquake of 1755. Nearby, on Rua Júlio Pereiro de Melo, the engaging **Museu do Mar** (☎ 214 815 906; Tues–Fri 10am–5pm, Sat & Sun 10am–1pm & 2–5pm; free) relates the town's relationship with the sea, with model boats, treasure from local wrecks and stuffed fish.

CASA DAS HISTÓRIAS

Avda da República 300 ☎ 214 826 970, ⊕ www .casadashistoriaspaularego.com. Tues–Sun 10am–6pm. €3. MAP BELOW

The distinctive ochre towers of the modernist **Casa das Histórias** mark a fantastic museum which, unusually, is dedicated to a living artist, Paula Rego. Designed by famous architect Eduardo Souto de Moura, the airy museum features over 120 of her disturbing but beautiful collages, pastels and engravings as well as those by her late English husband Victor Willing. Many of her works explore themes of power: women and animals are portrayed as both powerful and

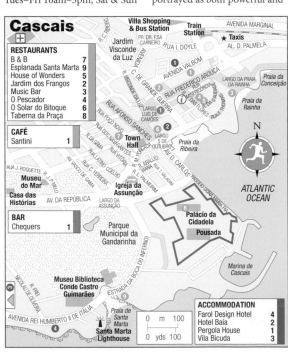

FISHING BOAT, CAPARICA

sexually vulnerable; men often appear as fish or dressed in women's clothes.

AROUND CASCAIS MARINA

MAP OPPOSITE

The leafy **Parque Municipal da Gandarinha**, complete with picnic tables and playground, makes a welcome escape from the beach crowds. In one corner stands the mansion of the nineteenth-century Count of Guimarães, preserved complete with its fittings as the **Museu Biblioteca Conde Castro Guimarães** (📞 214 825 401, 🖥 www.cm-cascais.pt; Tues–Sun 10am–5pm; closes 1–2pm on Sat and Sun; free). Its most valuable exhibits are rare illuminated sixteenth-century manuscripts.

PALÁCIO DA CIDADELA

Avda Dom Carlos I 📞 213 614 660, 🖥 www .cm-cascais.pt. Wed–Sun 2–8pm. €4
To the east, the walls of Cascais' largely seventeenth-century **Citadela** (fortress) guard the entrance to the **Marina de Cascais**, an enclave of expensive yachts serviced by restaurants, bars and boutiques.

Originally a sea fort and then a summer retreat for Portuguese royalty, the Citadela has been used by the Portuguese president to entertain his guests ever since the declaration of the Republic in 1910. Today, you can wander around the lower-floor exhibition space, though it's worth the entrance fee to visit the top two floors (ask for a non-guided visit unless you understand Portuguese). There's also a lovely tearoom facing the ocean.

CAPARICA

Via Rapida express 135 (roughly hourly; 30min) or slower local buses (every 15–30min; 50min), from Cacilhas or bus #161 from Lisbon's Areeiro (every 30–60min; 40–60min).
According to legend, Caparica was named after the discovery of a cloak (*capa*) full of golden coins. Today it is a slightly tacky, high-rise seaside resort, but don't let that put you off; it's family friendly, has plenty of good seafood as well as several kilometres of soft sandy beach. From the beach, a **narrow-gauge mini-railway** (June–Sept daily every 30min from 9am–7.30pm, last return 7pm; €7.50 return, or €4.50 return for first nine stops) runs south along the beach for 8km to the resort of **Fonte da Telha**. Jump off at any stop en route; earlier stops tend to be family oriented, while nudity is common in later ones.

CAPARICA BEACH

Restaurants

B & B

Rua do Poço Novo 15–17, Cascais ☎ 214 820 686. Mon–Sat noon–2.30pm & 6–9pm. MAP P.128
A small, intimate diner in the old town, specializing in tender steaks (around €13). Also does a few fresh fish dishes, omelettes and salads and great desserts – save room for the chocolate cake.

ESPLANADA SANTA MARTA

Avda Rei Humberto II de Italia, Cascais ☎ 961 577 902. Tues–Sat 10am–10pm. MAP P.128
One of the best places on the coast to enjoy charcoal-grilled fish and savouries (from €9), which are served on a tiny terrace overlooking the sea and a little beach. No credit cards.

HOUSE OF WONDERS

Largo da Misericordia 53 ☎ 911 702 428. Daily 10am–midnight. MAP P.128
This Dutch-run veggie café-restaurant and gallery space has an appealing, alternative vibe. The street-level restaurant serves amazing vegetarian meze of various sizes from €8–15. Expect hummus, chickpea salad and whatever fresh veg are in season. There's a separate entrance for the gallery space and laidback café, complete

with a little roof terrace where you can relax for a drink on old packing cases.

JARDIM DOS FRANGOS

Avda Com. Grande Guerra 68 ☎ 214 861 717, Cascais. Daily 10am–midnight. MAP P.128
Permanently buzzing with people and sizzling with the speciality, bargain grilled chicken from around €7, which is devoured by the plateful at indoor and outdoor tables. Get there early to guarantee a table as it is very popular.

MUSIC BAR

Largo Praia da Rainha 121, Cascais ☎ 214 820 848. June–Sept daily 10am–10pm; Oct–May closed Mon. MAP P.128
Great sea views are to be had inside or out on the raised terrace at this bustling café-restaurant. It's a fine spot to have a sunset beer. It also does decent, moderately priced fish, pasta and grilled meats (around €14–18).

O BARBAS CATEDRAL

Apoio de Praia 13, Caparica ☎ 212 900 163. Daily noon–midnight; Oct–April closes Wed.
Caparica's best-known beach restaurant with affordable fish, *caldeirada* and *arroz de marisco* to die for. They also run the more upmarket space next door, *O Barbas Tertúlia*, though the menu is much the same.

O PESCADOR

Rua das Flores 106, Cascais ☎ 214 832 054, ⓦ www.restaurantepescador.com. Mon 6.30–11pm, Tues–Sat noon–3pm & 6.30–11pm. MAP P.128

The best of a row of lively restaurants near the fish market, offering upmarket seafood – expect to pay over €25 for superb mains such as lobster baked in salt or tuna cooked in olive oil and garlic.

O SOLAR DO BITOQUE

Rua Regimento 19 de Infantaria Loja 11, Cascais ☎ 918 580 343. Mon–Sat 10am–midnight. MAP P.128

Bitoques are thin steaks, and this lively local with outdoor seating specializes in various types as well as burgers, salads and fresh fish. Very good value, with most dishes under €9.

PRAIA DO TAMARIZ

Praia do Tamariz, Estoril ☎ 214 681 010, ⓦ www.restaurantepraiadotamariz.com. Daily April–Oct 9am–10pm, Nov–March noon–6pm

High-profile restaurant right on the seafront promenade – which makes good-value fish, meat, pizza and pasta dishes (mains from €12–15). Also a great spot for a sangria or *caipirinha*.

TABERNA DA PRAÇA

Cidadela de Cascais, Avda Dom Carlos I ☎ 210 401 712. Mon–Sat noon–3pm & 7–11pm, Sun closes 10pm. MAP P.128

Tucked into a couple of cosy arched rooms within Cascais's impressive fortress, *Taberna da Praça* serves a range of tasty *petiscos*, the Portuguese version of tapas. You can sample regional specialities like scrambled eggs with smoked chicken chorizo, or grilled octopus with baked potatoes (€4–10). There are also more substantial mains: great tuna steaks or duck rice (from €14).

Café

SANTINI

Avda Valbom 28f ☎ 214 833 709. Daily 11am–midnight. MAP P.128

Opened by an Italian immigrant just after World War II, *Santini*'s delicious ice creams are legendary in these parts.

Bars and clubs

CHEQUERS

Largo Luís de Camões 7, Cascais ☎ 214 830 926. Daily 9.30–2am. MAP P.128

An English-style pub that fills up early with a good-time crowd; it serves so-so meals, too, with weekend DJs and live soccer on TV, though most people come for drinks at tables outside in the attractive square.

JONAS BAR

Passeio Marítimo, Praia das Moitas Monte Estoril ☎ 214 676 946. Mon–Sat 9am–midnight (closes earlier in winter in bad weather). MAP P.124

Right on the seafront just north of Estoril, this is a laidback spot day or night, selling cocktails, juices and snacks until the small hours.

JONAS BAR MONTE ESTORIL

Hotels and guesthouses

Lisbon's hotels range from sumptuous five-stars to backstreet hideaways packed with local character. The grander ones tend to be found along Avenida da Liberdade, around Parque Eduardo VII or out of the centre, though in recent years around forty have opened in the central Baixa where there are endless options. Besides hotels, there are guesthouses (*alojamento local* or *particular*, some of which keep the now abandoned titles of *pensão* or *residencial*) and various good-value hostels.

Prices given are for a night in the cheapest double room in high season. Rates drop considerably out of season. Unless otherwise stated, all the places reviewed below have an en-suite bath or shower and include breakfast (anything from bread, jam and coffee to a generous spread of rolls, cereals, croissants, cold meat, cheese and fruit).

The Baixa and Rossio

ALBERGARIA INSULANA > Rua da Assunção 52 Ⓜ Rossio ☎ 213 427 625, Ⓦ www.insulana.net. MAP P.33, POCKET MAP D12. Go upstairs past a series of shops to reach one of the more quirky Baixa options. With its own bar overlooking a quiet pedestrianized street, the hotel's slightly faded rooms are complete with satellite TV and a/c. English-speaking staff. **€66**

HOTEL AVENIDA PALACE > Rua 1º de Dezembro 123 Ⓜ Restauradores ☎ 213 218 100, Ⓦ www.hotelavenidapalace .pt. MAP P.33, POCKET MAP C11. Built at the end of the nineteenth century, and rumoured to have a secret door direct to neighbouring Rossio station, this is one of Lisbon's grandest hotels. Despite extensive modernization, the traditional feel has been maintained with chandeliers and period furniture throughout. There are 82 spacious rooms, each with high ceilings and colossal bathrooms. **€175**

HOTEL LISBOA TEJO > Rua dos Condes de Monsanto 2 Ⓜ Rossio ☎ 218 866 182, Ⓦ www.lisboatejohotel.com. MAP P.33, POCKET MAP E11. Not in the quietest of streets, but this historic Baixa townhouse has been given a stylish makeover, and now combines bare brickwork with cutting-edge design. Wood-floored rooms aren't huge but come with modems and minibars, and downstairs there is a boutiquey, Gaudí-inspired bar. **€95**

HOTEL MÉTROPOLE > Rossio 30, Ⓜ Restauradores ☎ 213 219 030, Ⓦ www.metropole-lisbon.com. MAP P.33, POCKET MAP D11. Early twentieth century-era three-star, with an airy lounge bar offering superb views over Rossio and the castle. The simply furnished but spacious rooms are comfortable, but the square can be quite noisy at night. **€135**

PENSÃO GERÊS > Calçada da Garcia 6 Ⓜ Rossio ☎ 218 810 497, Ⓦ www .residencial-geres.lisbon-hotel.net. MAP P.33, POCKET MAP D10. Set on a steep side street just off Rossio, the beautiful, tiled entrance hall and chunky wooden doors set the tone for one of the more glamorous central options. The simple rooms of varying sizes are minimally furnished, though all have TV and bathroom. Internet access on request; no breakfast. **€45**

Booking a room

The main tourist offices (see p.149) can provide accommodation lists, but won't reserve rooms for you. In the summer months, confirm a reservation at least a week in advance and get written confirmation; most owners understand English. Look out, too, for deals on hotel websites which are usually cheaper than walk-in rates.

PENSÃO PORTUENSE > Rua das Portas de Santo Antão 149–157 ⓜRestauradores ☎213 464 197, ⓦwww.pensaoportuense.com. MAP P.33. POCKET MAP J5. Singles, doubles and triples in a family-run guesthouse in a great position. Decently decorated, all rooms come with a/c and TV, and there's wi-fi access. **€75**

RESIDENCIAL FLORESCENTE > Rua das Portas do Santo Antão 99 ⓜRestauradores ☎213 426 609, ⓦwww.residencialflorescente.com. MAP P.33. POCKET MAP J5. The best guesthouse on this pedestrianized street. There's a large selection of air-conditioned rooms across four floors (some en-suite with TV), so if you don't like the look of the room you're shown – and some are very cramped – ask about alternatives. Street-facing rooms can be noisy. There is also a lounge plus internet access for a small fee. **€85**

VIP EXECUTIVE ÉDEN > Praça dos Restauradores 24 ⓜRestauradores ☎213 216 600, ⓦwww.viphotels.com. MAP P.33. POCKET MAP C10. Compact studios and apartments sleeping up to four people are available within the impressively converted Éden cinema. Get a ninth-floor apartment with a balcony and you'll have the best views and be just below the superb breakfast bar and rooftop pool. All come with dishwashers, microwaves and satellite TV. Disabled access. **Studios from €95**

The Sé, Castelo and Alfama

ALBERGARIA SENHORA DO MONTE > Calçada do Monte 39, Tram #28 ☎218 866 002, ⓦwww.albergariasenhorado monte.com. MAP PP.46–47, POCKET MAP L5. Comfortable, modern hotel in a sublime location with views of the castle and Graça convent from the south-facing rooms (avoid the north-facing ones), some of which have terraces. Breakfast is taken on the fourth-floor terrace. Free wi-fi and private parking are available. **€110**

THE KEEP > Costa do Castelo 74, Tram #12 ☎218 854 070. MAP PP.46–47, POCKET MAP F11. Superbly sited in its own view-laden terrace-garden just below the castle, this is justifiably one of the most popular budget places in the city. The 16 rooms are spartan but bright, though avoid the dingy basement room. Book in advance. No breakfast. **€60** for shared facilities, otherwise **€75**

MEMMO ALFAMA > Trav Merceeiras 27, Tram #28 ☎210 495 660, ⓦwww.memmoalfama.com. MAP PP.46–47, POCKET MAP F12. Hidden behind the facade of a former house, paint factory and bakery lies this sleek boutique hotel. Parts of the ground floor contain the old brick ovens, though the real appeal is the bar with terraces at the back, complete with small plunge pool, offering sumptuous views over the Alfama and the Tagus. Rooms are compact, but have all mod cons and most boast fine views. **€180**

PALACETE CHAFARIZ D'EL REI > Trav Chafariz d'El Rei 6, Tram #25 ☎218 886 150, ⓦwww.chafarizdelrei.com. MAP PP.46–47, POCKET MAP G12. Luxury guesthouse built in 1909 by a wealthy Brazilian merchant and lovingly restored a century later. From the reception – flooded with light from stained-glass windows – to the mirror room and library, the house is a stunning mix of Brazilian Art Nouveau and neo-Arabic flamboyance. Huge rooms, most with river views, have chandeliers and modern bathrooms while stonking breakfasts keep you going till dinner time. **€268**

SOLAR DO CASTELO > Rua das Cozinhas 2, Bus #37 ☎ 218 806 050, Ⓦ www.heritage.pt. MAP PP.46–47, POCKET MAP F11. A tastefully renovated eighteenth-century mansion abutting the castle walls on the site of the former palace kitchens, parts of which remain. Its 14 rooms cluster around a tranquil inner courtyard, where you can enjoy a vast buffet breakfast. Rooms aren't enormous, but most boast balconies overlooking the castle grounds, and service is second to none. **€140**

SOLAR DOS MOUROS Rua do Milagre de Santo António 6, Tram #28 ☎ 218 854 940, Ⓦ www.solardosmouros .com. MAP PP.46–47, POCKET MAP F12. A tall Alfama townhouse done out in a contemporary style with its own bar. Each of the twelve rooms offers fantastic vistas of the river (€60 extra) or castle and comes with CD player and a/c. There's plenty of modern art to enjoy if you tire of the view. **€100.**

Chiado and Cais do Sodré

HOTEL BAIRRO ALTO > Praça Luís de Camões 2 Ⓜ Baixa-Chiado ☎ 213 408 223, Ⓦ www.bairroaltohotel.com. MAP P.59, POCKET MAP C12. A grand eighteenth-century building that has been modernized into a fashionable boutique hotel. Rooms and communal areas still have a period feel – the lift takes a deep breath before rattling up its six floors – but modern touches appear in the form of DVDs in rooms, a hip rooftop café and a swish split-level bar full of comfy cushions. **€230**

HOTEL BORGES > Rua Garrett 108 Ⓜ Baixa-Chiado ☎ 213 461 951, Ⓦ www.hotelborges.com. MAP P.59, POCKET MAP C12. In a prime spot on

Chiado's main street, this traditional and elegantly furnished three-star is very popular, though front rooms can be noisy. Double or triple rooms are plain and small but good value. **€110**

HOTEL DO CHIADO > Rua Nova do Almada 114 Ⓜ Baixa-Chiado ☎ 213 256 100, Ⓦ www.hoteldochiado.pt. MAP P.59, POCKET MAP D12. Designed by architect Álvaro Siza Viera, this stylish hotel has lovely communal areas – orange segment-shaped windows give glimpses of Chiado in one direction and the whole city in the other. The cheapest rooms lack much of an outlook, but the best ones have terraces with stunning views towards the castle – a view you get from the bar terrace too. All rooms have wi-fi. Limited parking available. **€175**

LX BOUTIQUE > Rua do Alecrim 12 Ⓜ Cais do Sodré ☎ 213 474 394, Ⓦ www.lxboutiquehotel.pt. MAP P.59, POCKET MAP C13. A tasteful makeover to an old townhouse has made *LX Boutique* into a popular small hotel with its own chic restaurant. The *Boutique* refers to its themed floors named after Portuguese poets and fado singers. Rooms are all stylish and individual, with shutters and tasteful lighting – try and get one with river views rather than over the late-night Rua Nova do Carvalho. **€110**

Bairro Alto and São Bento

CASA DE SÃO MAMEDE > Rua da Escola Politécnica 159, Bus #1 ☎ 213 963 166, Ⓦ www.casadesaomamede .pt. MAP PP.68–69, POCKET MAP H5. On a busy street north of Príncipe Real, this is a superb eighteenth-century former magistrate's house with period fittings, bright breakfast room and a grand

---

Self-catering

There are several fine options for self-catering in Lisbon. As well as Ⓦ www .airbnb.co.uk, good first points of call are Ⓦ www.fadoflats.pt (mostly in Chiado and Alfama), Ⓦ www.castleinnlisbon.com, which has apartments right by the castle, or Ⓦ www.travellershouse.com, a hostel which also has four attractive apartments near Elevador da Lavra. Geared up to families is the upmarket Martinhal Chiado (Ⓦ www.martinhal.com) in the Chiado district.

Author picks

BUDGET *Home Hostel* p.141
DESIGNER *Memmo Alfama* p.135
RETRO CHIC *Heritage Avenida* p.138
FAMILY *Lisboa Plaza* p.139
HISTORIC *Palacete Chafariz d'el Rei* p.135

stained-glass window. Rooms are rather ordinary, but all are equipped with a TV and a/c. **€90**

HOTEL ANJO AZUL > Rua Luz Soriano 75, Bus #1 ☎ 213 478 069, Ⓦ www .blueangelhotel.com. MAP PP.68–69, POCKET MAP B11. The "Blue Angel" is best known for being gay friendly, but is not exclusively so. Set in a lovely blue-tiled townhouse right in the heart of the area's nightlife, there are 20 simple but attractive rooms set over four floors (€50), most with en-suite facilities (€65). No breakfast; however, there is a living room. **From €50**

HOTEL BELVER PRINCÍPE REAL > Rua da Alegria 53, Bus #1 ☎ 213 407 350, Ⓦ www.hotelprincipereal.belver hotels.net. MAP PP.68–69, POCKET MAP H5. This small four-star sits on a quiet street just below the Bairro Alto. Eighteen rooms, each with modern decor and some with balconies and superb city views. Best of all is the top-floor suite with stunning vistas (€180). **From €100**

THE INDEPENDENTE HOSTEL AND SUITES > Rua de São Pedro de Alcântara 81 ☎ 213 461 381, Ⓦ www .theindependente.pt. MAP PP.68–69, POCKET MAP B10. This is part hostel and part boutique hotel. The fantastic old building has far-reaching views over Lisbon. Lower floors house dorms (sleeping 6–12), each with towering ceilings. Upstairs are quirky double rooms in the roof spaces, the best with balconies offering river views. There's a downstairs bar and patio and the place offers everything from bar crawls and guided walks to cycle hire. The Suites element is in the building next door, offering larger rooms, a library and a hip bar on the roof terrace. **Dorms from €15, doubles and suites from €125**

PENSÃO GLOBO > Rua do Teixeira 37, Bus #1 ☎ 213 462 279, Ⓦ www .blueangelhotel.com/pensaoglobo. MAP PP.68–69, POCKET MAP B10. Attractive house on a relatively quiet street, bang in the middle of the Bairro Alto. Fifteen varied rooms: all are simple (including a box room for just €25), though avoid those without windows. There's a bar downstairs. No breakfast. **€40**

PENSÃO LONDRES > Rua Dom Pedro V 53, Bus #1 ☎ 213 462 203, Ⓦ www .pensaolondres.com.pt. MAP PP.68–69, POCKET MAP B10. Wonderful old building with high ceilings and 40 pleasant enough rooms sleeping up to four. Some have tiny bathrooms (€75); those without are cheaper (€45), and the best (ask for rooms 402, 409 or 411) have great views over the city. **From €45**

Estrela, Lapa and Santos

AS JANELAS VERDES > Rua das Janelas Verdes 47, Bus #727 or tram #25 ☎ 213 968 143, Ⓦ www.heritage .pt. MAP P.79, POCKET MAP G8. This discreet, eighteenth-century townhouse, where Eça de Queirós was inspired to write *Os Maias*, is just metres from the Museu de Arte Antiga. Spacious rooms come with marble bathrooms, period furnishings and most with views of the Tejo. Breakfast is served in the delightful walled garden in summer. The top-floor library and terrace command spectacular river views. **€130**

OLISSIPPO LAPA PALACE > Rua do Pau da Bandeira 4 ☎ 213 949 494, Ⓦ www.olissippolapapalacehotel .com. MAP P.79, POCKET MAP F7. A stunning nineteenth-century mansion set in its own lush gardens, with dramatic vistas over the Tejo. Rooms are luxurious, and those in the Palace Wing are each decorated in a different style, from Classical to Art Deco. There's also a health club, disabled access and a list of facilities as long as your arm, from babysitting to banqueting. **€380**

YORK HOUSE > Rua das Janelas Verdes 32, Bus #727 or tram #25 ☎ 213 962 435, Ⓦ www.yorkhouselisboa.com. MAP P.79, POCKET MAP G7. Located in a sixteenth-century Carmelite convent (and hidden from the main street by high walls), rooms here are chic and minimalist. The best are grouped around a beautiful interior courtyard, where drinks and meals are served in summer, and there's a highly rated restaurant. Advance bookings recommended. **€125**

Alcântara and Belém

JERÓNIMOS 8 > Rua das Jerónimos 8, Tram #15 ☎ 213 600 900, Ⓦ www .jeronimos8.com. MAP PP.92–93, POCKET MAP C4. In a great position for Belém's attractions, this hotel is an attractive stone building with boutiquey touches – crisp white decor, marble bathrooms and a modern bar area, plus a substantial buffet breakfast. **€210**

PESTANA PALACE > Rua Jau 54, Tram #18 ☎ 213 615 600, Ⓦ www.pestana .com. MAP PP.84–85, POCKET MAP C8. Set in an early twentieth-century palace full of priceless works of art, most beds at this five-star hotel are in tasteful modern wings that stretch either side of lush gardens. Most rooms have large terraces and lie a short walk from a sushi bar, a sunken outdoor pool with a fountain to swim out to, and an indoor pool and health club. The price, which can be greatly reduced for summer offers, includes a vast breakfast in the former ballroom. **€200**

Avenida, Parque Eduardo VII and the Gulbenkian

CASA AMORA > Rua João Penha 13 Ⓜ Rato ☎ 919 300 317, Ⓦ www .casaamora.com. MAP PP.100–101, POCKET MAP G5. This lovingly renovated townhouse lies close to the picturesque Praça das Amoreiras. There are five tastefully furnished rooms in the main house and six larger studios in a separate building which are suitable for families. There's also an attractive outdoor patio. Rooms **€135**, studios from **€145**

DOUBLE TREE FONTANA PARK > Rua Eng. Viera da Silva 2 Ⓜ Saldanha ☎ 210 410 600, Ⓦ www.doubletree3

.hilton.com. MAP PP.100–101, POCKET MAP J3. This buzzy designer hotel rises sleekly behind the facade of an old steelworks. Chic rooms – the best with terraces – come with Philippe Starck chromatic baths. The communal areas include a restaurant, bar and a courtyard garden with slate walls of running water. Cocktail and sushi nights with guest DJs complete the picture. **€160**

EUROSTAR DAS LETRAS > Rua Castilho 6–12 Ⓜ Avenida ☎ 213 573 094, Ⓦ www.eurostarshotels.com. MAP PP.100–101, POCKET MAP H5. Modern hotel with its own small gym and bar in a good position between the centre and the Bairro Alto. Rooms come with comfy beds, a choice of pillows and a complicated array of power showers. The best have balconies with downtown views. **€130**

HERITAGE AVENIDA LIBERDADE > Avda da Liberdade Ⓜ Restauradores ☎ 213 404 040, Ⓦ www.heritage.pt. MAP PP.100–101, POCKET MAP J5. In a fine mansion – whose ground floor once sold herbal remedies (the counter still remains) – this hotel superbly blends tradition and contemporary style. Though the dining area/bar is small (and the gym/plunge pool even smaller), the rooms more than compensate with retro fittings and great cityscapes from top-floor rooms. **€148**

HOTEL AVENIDA PARK > Avda Sidónio Pais 6 Ⓜ Parque ☎ 213 532 181, Ⓦ www.avenidapark.com. MAP PP.100–101, POCKET MAP H4 Good-sized rooms – beg for one with a view over the park for no extra charge – in a friendly, if dated, hotel on a quiet street. **€90**

HOTEL BRITANIA > Rua Rodrigues Sampaio 17 Ⓜ Avenida ☎ 213 155 016, Ⓦ www.heritage.pt. MAP PP.100–101, POCKET MAP J5. Designed in the 1940s by influential architect Cassiano Branco, this is an Art Deco gem with huge airy rooms, each with traditional cork flooring and marble-clad bathrooms. The hotel interior, with library and bar, has been declared of national architectural importance. A somewhat pricey breakfast is an extra. **€160**

HOTEL DOM CARLOS PARQUE > Avda Duque de Loulé 121 Ⓜ Marquês de Pombal ☎ 213 512 590, Ⓦ www .domcarloshoteis.com. MAP PP.100–101, POCKET MAP H4. Decent three-star just off Praça Marquês de Pombal, with fair-sized rooms over eight floors, each with cable TV. Some overlook the neighbouring police and fire stations, which can add to the noise. There's a downstairs bar with plasma TV and garage parking. **€96**

INSPIRA SANTA MARTA > Rua de Santa Marta 48 ☎ 210 440 900, Ⓦ www.inspirahotels.com. MAP PP.100–101, POCKET MAP J4. The facade of a traditional townhouse hides a modern boutique hotel which boasts impressive green credentials, including low energy lighting and recycled or local products. Feng shui-designed rooms are compact but comfy with glass-wall showers, coffee-making facilities and free minibars. There is also a spa, a games room, a stylish restaurant and bar. **€125**

LISBOA PLAZA > Trav Salitre 7 Ⓜ Avenida ☎ 213 218 218, Ⓦ www .hcritage.pt. MAP PP.100–101, POCKET MAP J5. A tasteful, understated former Portuguese family home with marble bathrooms, bar and a fashionable rooftop terrace, a short walk from the main Avenida. Friendly staff and good for families. Limited disabled access. **€110**

NH LIBERDADE > Avda da Liberdade 180b Ⓜ Avenida ☎ 213 514 060, Ⓦ www.nh-hotels.com. MAP PP.100–101, POCKET MAP J5. Discreetly tucked into the back of the Tivoli forum shopping centre off the main Avenida, this Spanish chain hotel offers ten floors of modern flair. The best rooms have balconies facing the traditional Lisbon houses at the back. Unusually for central Lisbon, there's a rooftop pool. There's also a bar and restaurant. **€166**

RESIDENCIAL ALEGRIA > Praça da Alegria 12 Ⓜ Avenida ☎ 213 220 670, Ⓦ www.alegrianet.com. MAP PP.100–101, POCKET MAP J5. Friendly place in a great position, facing the leafy Praça da Alegria ("Happy Square"). Spacious, brightly coloured rooms with TV, though front ones can be noisy. No breakfast. **€83**

SANA REX > Rua Castilho 169 Ⓜ Marquês de Pombal/Parque ☎ 213 882 161, Ⓦ www.rex.sanahotels.com. MAP PP.100–101, POCKET MAP G4. One of the less outrageously priced hotels in this neck of the woods with small but well-equipped rooms, a bar and its own restaurant. The best rooms are at the front, sporting large balconies overlooking Parque Eduardo VII. **€75**

SHERATON LISBOA > Rua Latino Coelho 1 Ⓜ Picoas ☎ 213 120 000, Ⓦ www.sheratonlisboa.com. MAP PP.100–101, POCKET MAP J3. This 1970s high-rise is something of an icon in this part of Lisbon and a mecca for those seeking five-star spa facilities. The dated exterior hides modern attractions including a heated outdoor pool, swanky rooms and a top floor bar and restaurant. **€150**

Sintra

CASA DO VALLE > Rua da Paderna 2 ☎ 219 244 699, Ⓦ www.casadovalle .com. MAP P.117. Though steeply downhill from the historic centre, this charming guesthouse still commands unbeatable views across the wooded slopes of Sintra. There are various rooms, from top-floor doubles with the best views, to ground-floor rooms with their own terraces. All rooms access a beautiful garden with its own pool. Good for families. **€90.** Breakfast **€6** extra

CHALET RELOGIO > Estrada da Pena 22, Sintra-Vila ☎ 963 966 325. MAP P.117. Architect Luigi Mannini, who worked on the Quinta da Regaleira (see p.119), designed this mansion with a distinctive clock tower. Rooms are simply furnished but enormous, with big windows and high ceilings, and there's a garden too, though it's a long walk to town and you'll need a car. **€75**

CHALET SAUDADE > Rua Dr. Alfredo Costa 21 ☎ 710 150 055, Ⓦ saudade .pt. MAP P.117. This tall eighteenth-century chalet has been superbly renovated by a Portuguese couple who have retained many of the quirky but charming original fittings. The interior is all parquet flooring, swirling stairways, stained glass and beautiful *azulejos*. Stairs take you down three floors to rooms of varying sizes: it's best to pay €10 extra to bag the one opening onto the garden. Breakfast (€10 extra) is offered at *Saudade Café* (see p.125). **€70**

HOTEL ARRIBAS > Avda A Coelho 28, Praia Grande ☎ 219 289 050, ⓦ www .hotelarribas.pt. MAP P.117. This three-star is plonked ungraciously above the beach. Faded but giant rooms come with minibars and satellite TV – those with a sea view are hard to fault. There are also seawater swimming pools, a restaurant and café terrace. Has family rooms sleeping up to four. Disabled access. **€120**

HOTEL NOVA SINTRA > Largo Afonso de Albuquerque 25, Estefânia ☎ 219 230 220, ⓦ www.novasintra.com. MAP P.117. A friendly hotel in a big mansion, whose elevated terrace-café overlooks a busy street. The modern rooms all have cable TV and shiny marble floors, and there's a decent restaurant. **€95**

HOTEL SINTRA JARDIM > Trav dos Avelares 12, São Pedro ☎ & ⓕ 219 230 738, ⓦ www.hotelsintrajardim .pt. MAP P.117. The best mid-range option in the area, this rambling old hotel has soaring ceilings, wooden floors and oodles of character. There's a substantial garden with a swimming pool and the giant rooms can easily accommodate extra beds – so it's great for families. Book ahead in summer; in winter there's a log fire in the communal lounge. **€80, €10 extra for garden views**

SÃO SATURNIA > Azóia ☎ 219 289 686, ⓦ www.saosat.com. MAP P.117. Reached down a steep track – look for the sign left just past the turning to Cabo da Roca, before Azóia – this former convent dates back to the twelfth century and sits in a valley where time seems to stand still. The six rooms, three suites and self-catering apartment are traditionally furnished, while the rambling communal areas are all weathered beams, bare bricks and low ceilings. There's a small outdoor pool, barbecue area, geese, cats, and terraces with stunning views – truly magical. **€140**

Lisbon coast

FAROL DESIGN HOTEL > Avda Rei Humberto II de Italia 7, Cascais ☎ 214 823 490, ⓦ www.farol.com.pt. MAP P.128. Right on the seafront, this is one of the area's most fashionable hideaways, neatly combining traditional and contemporary architecture. A new designer wing has been welded onto a sixteenth-century villa, and the decor combines wood and marble with modern steel and glass. The best rooms have sea views and terraces. There's also a restaurant, fairy-lit outside bar and seapool facing a fine rocky foreshore. **€264/320 with sea views**

HOTEL BAÍA > Avda Marginal, Cascais ☎ 214 831 033, ⓦ www.hotel baia.com. MAP P.128. Large seafront hotel boasting 113 rooms with a/c and satellite TV; front ones have balconies overlooking the beach. There's a great rooftop terrace complete with a covered pool, and a good restaurant. Parking charged extra. **€125/140 with sea view**

PERGOLA HOUSE > Avda Valbom 13, Cascais ☎ 214 840 040, ⓦ www .pergolahouse.pt. MAP P.128. Sumptuous century-old mansion bang in the centre of town with its own garden, stucco ceilings and wonderfully ornate tiled dining room. Each room has its own distinct character, some with their own balconies. **€135**

REAL CAPARICA HOTEL > Rua Mestre Manuel 18, Caparica ☎ 212 918 870, ⓦ www.realcaparicahotel.com. Friendly and reasonable central hotel, a few minutes' walk from the beach, just off Rua dos Pescadores. Small but pleasant rooms come with TV and bath and some have balconies and sea views. **€50**

VILA BICUDA > Rua dos Faisões, Cascais ☎ 214 860 200, ⓦ www .vilabicuda.com. MAP P.128. A very well run, upmarket villa complex set in its own grounds with two large swimming pools. Excellent for families, the modern villas are well equipped and the complex has its own great café, shop and (pricey) Italian restaurant. But you'll need a car – it's around 3km from central Cascais towards Guincho. **Studios from €146**

Hostels

Lisbon and its surroundings have some of Europe's best independent hostels. A youth hostel card is required for the official Portuguese hostels (*pousadas de juventude*), but you can buy one on your first night's stay. Unless stated, prices do not include breakfast.

HOME HOSTEL > Rua de São Nicolau 13-2 ☎ 218 885 312, Ⓦ www.home lisbonhostel.com. MAP P.33, POCKET MAP E12. In the heart of the Baixa, this highly rated hostel comes with fantastic home-cooking, a buzzy communal lounge and the opportunity to sign up to walking tours and pub nights. Four, six or eight-bed dorms from €22

LISBON LOUNGE HOSTEL > Rua de São Nicolau 41 Ⓜ Rossio ☎ 213 462 061, Ⓦ www.lisbonloungehostel.com. MAP P.33, POCKET MAP D12. A popular independent hostel in a great old Baixa townhouse full of stripped floorboards, comfy sofas and books. Free wi-fi and breakfast and dinner on request. Dorm beds from €22, twins from €32

LISBON POET'S HOSTEL > Rua Nova da Trindade 2–5° Ⓜ Baixa-Chiado ☎ 213 461 241, Ⓦ www.lisbonpoetshostel.com. MAP P.59, POCKET MAP C12. On the fourth and fifth floors of a traditional townhouse, this arty hostel has a range of rooms. Compact dorms sleep four or six and there are also decent-sized doubles (€10 extra for en suite). You can help yourself to books and DVDs; free wi-fi and evening meals on request. Dorms from €25, doubles from €60

MOON HILL HOSTEL > Rua Guilherme Gomes Fernandes 17, Sintra ☎ 969 831 095, Ⓦ www.moonhillhostel.com. MAP P.117. This fantastic hostel has friendly staff, stylish decor and a range of contemporary rooms from en-suite doubles to dorms with bunk beds. There's a communal kitchen and lounge with a wood burner for the winter and a terrace and patio to unwind in the summer. Dorms from €20; doubles from €60

OASIS HOSTEL > Rua Santa Catarina 24 Ⓜ Baixa-Chiado/Tram #28 ☎ 213 478 044, Ⓦ www.oasislisboa.com. MAP PP.68–69, POCKET MAP A12. In a lovely townhouse with its own patio garden, this independent hostel is a stone's throw from the fashionable Miradouro Santa Catarina. Dorm beds from €24, doubles from €71

POUSADA DE JUVENTUDE DE CATALAZETE > Estrada Marginal, Oeiras ☎ 214 430 638, Ⓦ www.pousadas juventude.pt. This hostel is set in an eighteenth-century sea-fort overlooking the sea pools in Oeiras, a suburb on the train line to Cascais. Reception is open 8am to midnight. Parking available. Dorm beds from €13, twin rooms from €38

POUSADA DE JUVENTUDE DE LISBOA > Rua Andrade Corvo 46 Ⓜ Picoas ☎ 213 532 696, Ⓦ www.pousadas juventude.pt. MAP PP.100–101, POCKET MAP H3. The main city hostel, set in a rambling old building, with a small bar (open 6pm to midnight), canteen, TV room and disabled access. There are 30 dorms sleeping four to six as well as en-suite rooms. Price includes breakfast. Dorm beds from €17, doubles from €42

POUSADA DE JUVENTUDE LISBOA PARQUE DAS NAÇÕES > Rua de Moscavide 47–101, Parque das Nações Ⓜ Oriente ☎ 218 920 890, Ⓦ www .pousadasjuventude.pt. MAP P.111, POCKET MAP A16. About five minutes' walk northeast of the Torre Vasco da Gama, towards the bridge, this smart, modern youth hostel has a pool table and disabled access. Dorm beds from €17, doubles from €42

TRAVELLERS HOUSE > Rua Augusta 89-1° Ⓜ Baixa-Chiado ☎ 210 115 922, Ⓦ www.travellershouse.com. MAP P.33, POCKET MAP D12. Right on Lisbon's main pedestrianized street, this award-winning independent hostel has a wonderful lounge, bean bags and a DVD room and appealing en-suite doubles. Dorm beds from €22, doubles and studios from €70

Arrival

Lisbon airport is right on the edge of the city and is well served by buses and taxis. The city's train stations are all centrally located and connected to the metro; the main bus station is also close to metro and train stops.

By plane

The Aeroporto da Portela (☎ 218 413 500, ⓦ www.ana.pt) is a twenty-minute drive north of the city centre and has a tourist office (☎ 218 450 660; daily 7am–midnight), a 24hr exchange bureau and left-luggage facilities.

The easiest way in to the centre is by **taxi**; a journey to Rossio should cost around €15. The airport is also on the red Oriente line of the **metro** (see opposite), although you'll neeed to change at Alameda for the centre. Alternatively, catch Line 1 **Aerobus** (☎ 966 298 558, ⓦ www.yellowbus tours.com; daily every 20–30min, from 7am–11:20pm, €3.50, ticket valid for travel on all city buses for that day) from outside the terminal, which runs to Praça dos Restauradores, Rossio, Praça do Comércio and Cais do Sodré train station. **Local bus** #744 also runs to Praça Marquês de Pombal (every 10–15min; €1.80), but is less convenient if you have a lot of luggage.

By train

Long-distance **trains** are run by CP (Comboios de Portugal; ☎ 707 210 220 or ☎ 351 707 210 220 from abroad, ⓦ www.cp.pt). You'll arrive at Santa Apolónia station, from where you can access the Gaivota metro line or take a bus west to Praça do Comércio. Some trains stop at Entrecampos (on the Amarela line) or at Oriente station (on the Oriente line) at Parque das Nações. These stations are more convenient for the airport or northern Lisbon.

By bus

The national **bus** carrier is Rede Expressos (☎ 707 223 344, ⓦ www .rede-expressos.pt). Most services terminate at Sete Rios, next to the Jardim Zoológico metro stop (for the centre) and Sete Rios train line (for Sintra and the northern suburbs). Some bus services also stop at the Oriente station at Parque das Nações on the Oriente metro line.

By car

Apart from weekends, when the city is quiet, **driving** round Lisbon is best avoided, though it is useful to hire a car to see the outlying sights. Parking is difficult in central Lisbon. Pay-and-display spots get snapped up quickly and the unemployed get by on tips for guiding drivers into empty spots. It may be easier heading for an official car park, for which you pay around €2.50 an hour or €15 a day. Do not leave valuables inside your car.

Getting around

Central Lisbon is compact enough to explore on **foot**, but don't be fooled by the apparent closeness of sights as they appear on maps. There are some very steep hills to negotiate, although the city's quirky *elevadores* (funicular railways) will save you the steepest climbs. Tram, bus and *elevador* stops are indicated by a sign marked "paragem", which carries route details.

Metro stations (ⓜ) are located close to most of the main sights. Suburban trains run from Rossio and Sete Rios stations to Sintra and from Cais do Sodré station to Belém, Estoril and Cascais, while ferries (☎ 213 500 115, ⓦ www.transtejo .pt) link Lisbon's Cais do Sodré to Cacilhas, for the resort of Caparica.

The metro

Lisbon's efficient **metro** (Metropolitano; daily 6.30–1am; ☎ 213 500 115, ⊛ www.metro.transporteslisboa.pt) is the quickest way of reaching the city's main sights, with trains every few minutes. Tickets cost €1.40 per journey, or €1.25 with a Viva Viagem card (see below) – sold at all stations (see the inside cover and pull-out map for the network diagram).

Buses and trams

City trams and buses (daily 6.30am –midnight) are operated by Carris (☎ 213 500 115, ⊛ www.transporteslisboa.pt). **Buses** (autocarros) run just about everywhere in the Lisbon area – the most useful ones are outlined in the box below.

Trams (eléctricos) run on five routes, which are marked on the chapter maps. Ascending some of the steepest urban gradients in the world, most are worth taking for the ride alone, especially the cross-city tram #28 (see p.53). Another picturesque route is #12, which circles the castle area via Largo Martim Moniz. Other useful routes are "supertram" #15 from Praça da Figueira to Belém (signed Algés), and #18, which runs from Cais do Sodré via Praça do Comércio to the Palácio da Ajuda. The remaining route, #25, runs from near the Mercado da Ribeira to Campo Ourique via Santos, Lapa and Estrela.

Elevadores

There are also several **elevadores**. These consist of two funicular railways offering quick access to the heights of the Bairro Alto (see p.60 & p.66) and to the eastern side of Avenida da Liberdade (p.39); and one giant lift, the Elevador da Santa Justa (see p.37) which goes up to the foot of the Bairro Alto near Chiado. There are also free street lifts offering access to the lower edges of the Castelo de São Jorge (see map, pp.46–47).

Tickets and passes

On board **tickets** cost €1.80 (buses), €2.85 (trams) and €3.60 for elevadores (valid for two trips) and €5 for the Elevador da Santa Justa. You need to get a separate card for train lines to Sintra or Cascais. Note that the modern tram #15 has an automatic ticket machine on board and does not issue change.

It's possible just to buy a ticket each time you ride, but **passes**, available from any main metro station, can save you money. First, buy a rechargeable Viva Viagem card (€0.50), which you can load up with up to €2–15, after which €1.25 is deducted for each bus or metro journey.

You can also buy a one-day Bilhete 1dia pass (€6), which allows unlimited travel on buses, trams, the metro and elevadores for 24 hours after it is first used.

If you're planning some intensive sightseeing, the Cartão Lisboa (⊛ www.lisboacard.org; €18.50 for one day, €31.50 for two days, €39 for three, valid for one year) is a good buy. The card entitles you to unlimited rides on buses, trams,

---

Useful bus routes

#201 Night bus from Cais do Sodré to the docks via Santos; until 5am.

#728 Belém to Parque das Nações via Santa Apolónia station.

#737 Praça da Figueira to Castelo de São Jorge via the Sé and Alfama.

#744 Outside the airport to Marquês de Pombal via Saldanha and Picoas (for the youth hostel).

#727 Marquês de Pombal to Belém via Santos and Alcântara.

#773 Rato to Alcântara via Príncipe Real, Estrela and Lapa.

Sightseeing tours

Open-top bus tour The 1hr 40min "Circuito Tejo" (June–Sept every 15min 9am–6pm; Oct–May every 20min 9am–5.30pm; €16) takes passengers around Lisbon's principal sights; a day-ticket allows you to get on and off whenever you want. The "Olisipo" tour (June–Sept every 30min 9.15am–7.15pm; Oct–May every 30min 9.15 am–5.45pm; €16) takes in the Parque das Nações (see p.110). These and other tours depart from Praça da Figueira. (Information ☎ 213 478 030, ⓦ www.yellowbustours.com.)

Tourist tram tours The "Elétrico das Colinas" (Hills Tour) takes passengers on a ninety-minute ride in an early twentieth-century tram (June–Sept every 25min 9.30am–7pm; Oct–May every 30min 9.30am–5.30pm; €19), departing from Praça do Comércio and touring around Alfama, Chiado and the Bairro Alto. (Information on ☎ 213 478 030, ⓦ www.yellowbustours.com.)

River cruises Various rib rides can be booked from alongside the Padrão dos Descobrimentos in Belém, including one-hour rides to below the Alfama (€35) or forty-minute high-speed tours (€40). (Information ☎ 933 924 740, ⓦ www.lisbonbyboat.com.)

Jeep tours Head round the city in a Portuguese-built, open-top military jeep, able to negotiate some of the city's tortuous hills and alleys that buses can't reach. Various tours from €40 (☎ 913 776 598, ⓦ www .wehatetourismtours.com.)

Walks Recommended themed two- to three-hour guided walks are offered by Lisbon Walker (☎ 218 861 840, ⓦ www.lisbonwalker.com; €15), departing daily from Praça do Comércio at 10am or 2.30pm, giving expert insight into the quirkier aspects of the city's sites including secret histories and spies.

Tuk-tuk tours Various companies offer tours in three-wheeled tuk-tuks that can negotiate Lisbon's steepest and narrow streets around the Alfama. Prices start at around €40 an hour and depart from outside the Sé cathedral and also Sintra train station.

elevadores and the metro as well as entry to or discounts on around 25 museums. It's available online and from all the main tourist offices.

Taxis

Lisbon's cream **taxis** have a minimum charge of €2; an average ride across town is €10–15. Fares are twenty percent higher from 9pm to 6am, at weekends and on public holidays. Bags in the boot incur a €1.60 fee. Meters should be switched on, and tips are not expected. Outside the rush hour taxis can be flagged down quite easily, or head for one of the ranks such as those outside the main train stations. At night, it's best to phone a taxi (attracts an extra charge of €0.80): try Teletaxis (☎ 218 111 100, ⓦ teletaxis.pt).

Car rental

For more information on driving in Lisbon see p.144. Rental agents include: Auto Jardim, ☎ 213 549 182, airport ☎ 218 463 187, ⓦ www.auto-jardim.com; Avis, ☎ 213 514 560, airport ☎ 218 435 550, ⓦ www.avis .com; Budget, ☎ 213 514 560, airport ☎ 213 195 555, ⓦ www.budget.com .pt; Europcar, ☎ 213 475 502, airport ☎ 218 401 176, ⓦ www.europcar .com; Hertz, ☎ 808 202 038, airport ☎ 219 426 300, ⓦ www.hertz.com.

Directory A–Z

Addresses

Addresses are written in the form "Rua do Crucifixo 50 4°", meaning the fourth storey of no. 50, Rua do Crucifixo. The addition of e, d or r/c at the end means the entrance is on the left (*esquerda*), right (*direita*) or on the ground floor (*rés-do-chão*).

Bike hire

Most of Lisbon is very hilly, but the riverfront is flat and good for bike hire. There are bike hire outlets at Belém (see p.90) and Doca de Santo Amaro (Armazém 7 ☎218 250 266, ⓦwww.slowfastcycles.com, daily 10am–7pm). Expect to pay around €5 an hour.

Cinemas

Mainstream **films** are shown at various multiplexes around the city, usually with Portuguese subtitles. Listings can be found on ⓦ www.agendalx.pt /cinema. The Instituto da Cinemateca Portuguesa, Rua Barata Salgueiro 39 ⓜAvenida (☎ 213 596 200, ⓦwww .cinemateca.pt), the national film theatre, has twice-daily shows and contains its own cinema museum.

Crime

Violent crime is very rare but pickpocketing is common, especially on public transport.

Electricity

Portugal uses two-pin plugs (220/240v). UK appliances will work with a continental adaptor.

Embassies and consulates

Australia, Avenida da Liberdade 200° ⓜAvenida; ☎ 213 101 500; Canada, Avenida da Liberdade 198–200-3° ⓜAvenida; ☎ 213 164 600; Ireland, Avenida da Liberdade 200-4° ⓜAvenida; ☎ 213 308 200; South

Emergencies

For police, fire and ambulance services, dial ☎ 112

Africa, Avda Luís Bivar 10 ⓜPicoas; ☎ 213 192 200; UK, Rua de São Bernardo 33 ⓜRato; ☎ 213 924 000, ⓦ www.gov.uk/government/world/ portugal; US, Avenida das Forças Armadas, ⓜJardim Zoológico; ☎217 273 300.

Events listings

The best listings magazine is the free monthly *Agenda Cultural* (ⓦwww .agendalx.pt) produced by the town hall (in Portuguese). *Follow me Lisboa* is an English-language version produced by the local tourist office. Both are available from the tourist offices and larger hotels.

Gay and lesbian travellers

The Centro Comunitário Gay e Lésbico de Lisboa at Rua de Sao Lázaro 88 (☎ 218 873 918; Fri & Sat 6–11pm; ⓜ Martim Moniz) is the main gay and lesbian community centre, run by ILGA, whose website (ⓦ www.ilga -portugal.pt) is in Portuguese.

Health

Pharmacies, the first point of call if you are ill, are open Mon–Fri 9am–1pm & 3–7pm, Sat 9am 1pm. Details of **24hr pharmacies** are posted on every pharmacy door, or call ☎118. The most central hospital is Hospital de Santa Maria (Avenida Prof. Egas Moniz ☎217 805 000, ⓦwww .chln.min-saude.pt). There are various other public hospitals around the city; EU citizens will need form E112.

Internet

Most hotels offer free wi-fi and often have computers for public use in reception. Most large cafés, bars and restaurants also offer free wi-fi.

Left luggage

There are 24hr lockers at the airport, main train and bus station, charging around €8 per day.

Lost property

Report any loss to the **tourist police** station in the Foz Cultura building in Palácio Foz, Praça dos Restauradores (daily 24hr ☎ 213 421 634). For items left on public transport, contact Carris ☎ 218 535 403.

Money

Portugal uses the **euro** (€). Banks open Monday to Friday 8.30am–3pm. Most central branches have automatic exchange machines for various currencies. You can withdraw up to €400 per day from ATMs ("Multibanco") with a maximum €200 per transaction – check fees with your home bank.

Opening hours

Most **shops** open Monday to Saturday 9am–7pm; smaller shops close for lunch (around 1–3pm) and on Saturday afternoons; shopping centres are open daily until 10pm or later. Most **museums** and **monuments** open Tuesday to Sunday from around 10am–6pm; details are given in the Guide.

Opera

Lisbon's main opera house is the Rococo Teatro Nacional São Carlos (Rua Serpa Pinto 9 ☎ 213 253 045, ⓦ www.tnsc.pt).

Phones

Most European-subscribed **mobile phones** will work in Lisbon, though you are likely to be charged extra for incoming and outgoing calls. The cheap rate for national and international calls is 9pm–9am Monday to Friday, and all day weekends and public holidays.

Post

Post offices (*correios*) are usually open Monday to Friday 8.30am–6.30pm. The main Lisbon office at Praça dos Restauradores 58 is open until 10pm, and 9am–6pm at weekends (☎ 213 238 971). Stamps (*selos*) are sold at post offices and anywhere that has the sign "Correio de Portugal – Selos" displayed.

Smoking

In common with most other EU countries, smoking is prohibited in most restaurants and cafés.

Sports

Lisbon boasts two of Europe's top **football** teams (see p.106), Benfica (ⓦ www.slbenfica.pt) and Sporting (ⓦ www.sporting.pt). Fixtures and news on ⓦ www.ligaportugal.pt. The area also contains some of Europe's best **golf courses**, especially around Cascais and Estoril (info at ⓦ www.portugalgolfe.pt). The Atlantic beaches at Caparica and Guincho are ideal for **surfing** and windsurfing, and international competitions are frequently held there (details on ⓦ www.surfing portugal.com). **Horseriding** is superb in the Sintra hills, and skilled horsemanship can also be seen at Portuguese **bullfights** (see Praça de Touros, p.105). The Estoril Open in April/May draws **tennis** fans to the city (ⓦ www .millenniumestorilopen.com), and thousands of runners hit the streets for the **Lisbon Marathon** (ⓦ www .maratonclubedeportugal.com), held in September/October.

Tickets

You can **buy tickets** for Lisbon's theatres and many concerts from the ticket desk in FNAC (ⓦ www .fnac.pt) in the Armazéns do Chiado shopping centre (see p.62), as well as from the main venues themselves. Online tickets can be purchased from ⓦ www.ticketline.sapo.pt or ⓦ blueticket.pt.

Time

Portuguese **time** is the same as Greenwich Mean Time (GMT). Clocks go forward an hour in late March and back to GMT in late October.

Tipping

Service charges are included in hotel and restaurant bills. A ten-percent tip is usual for restaurant bills, and hotel porters and toilet attendants expect at least €0.50.

Toilets

There are very few **public toilets** in the streets, although they can be found in nearly all main tourist sights (signed variously as *casa de banho*, *retrete*, *banheiro*, *lavabos* or "WC"), or sneak into a café or restaurant if need be. Gents are usually marked "H" (*homens*) or "C" (*cabalheiros*), and ladies "M" (*mulheres*) or "S" (*senhoras*).

Tourist information

Lisbon's main **tourist office** is the Lisbon Welcome Centre at Praça do Comércio (see map on p.33; daily 9am–8pm; ☎ 210 312 810, ⓦ www .visitlisboa.com), which can supply accommodation lists, bus timetables and maps. The main Portugal tourist office at Palácio Foz, Praça dos Restauradores (daily 9am–8pm; ☎ 213 463 314, ⓦ www.askmelisboa .com), is also helpful.

Tourist offices at the airport (see p.144) and at Santa Apolónia station (Mon–Sat 8am–1pm & 2–4pm; ☎ 218 821 606) can help you find accommodation, as can a few smaller "Ask Me" kiosks dotted around town, like the one opposite

Belém's Mosteiro dos Jerónimos (daily 10am–6pm). There is also the Y Lisboa tourist office at Rua Jardim do Regedor 50 (daily 10am–7pm; ☎ 213 472 134), with information geared to young and student travellers.

There are also tourist offices in all the main **day-trip destinations**: Sintra Turismo (see map, p.117; daily 9.30am–6pm, until 7pm in August; ☎ 219 231 157, ⓦ www.cm-sintra .pt); Cascais Turismo (Largo Cidade Vitória; daily 9am–6pm; ☎ 912 034 214, ⓦ www.visitcascais.com); and Caparica Turismo (Frente Urbana de Praias; Mon–Sat 9.30am–1pm & 2–5.30pm, closed Sat from Oct–March; ☎ 212 900 071, ⓦ www .m-almada.pt)

Travel agents

The well-informed Top Atlântico, Rua do Ouro 109 (☎ 218 646 575, ⓦ www .topatlantico.pt), Raixa, also acts as an American Express agent.

Travellers with disabilities

Lisbon airport offers a service for **wheelchair-users** if advance notice is given to your airline (details on ⓦ www.ana.pt, ☎ 218 413 500), while the Orange Badge symbol is recognized for disabled car parking. The main public transport company, Carris, offers an inexpensive dial-a-ride minibus service, O Serviço Mobilidade Reduzida especial, (€1.80 per trip; Mon–Fri 6.30am–9.30pm, Sat & Sun 8am–noon & 2–6pm; ☎ 213 613 141, ⓦ www.carris.pt), though two days' advance notice and a medical certificate are required.

Water

Lisbon's **water** is technically safe to drink, though you may prefer bottled water. Inexpensive bottled water is sold in any supermarket, though tourist shops and restaurants charge considerably more.

Festivals and events

CARNIVAL

February–March
Brazilian-style parades and costumes, mainly at Parque das Nações.

PEIXE EM LISBOA

March–April Ⓦ www.peixemlisboa.com
Lisbon's annual fish festival takes place at the Pátio da Galé in Praça do Comércio and includes masterclasses by top chefs.

SINTRA MUSIC FESTIVAL

May Ⓦ www.festivaldesintra.pt
Performances by international orchestras and dance groups in and around Sintra, Estoril and Cascais.

ROCK IN RIO LISBOA

May (even yearly) Ⓦ www.rockinrio-lisboa.sapo.pt
Five-day mega rock festival in Parque Bela Vista, in the north of the city.

SANTOS POPULARES

June
June sees a series of city-wide events loosely based around three saints' days. Lisbon's main festival is for its adopted saint, Santo António. On June 12 there's a parade down Avenida da Liberdade followed by a giant street party in the Alfama, and the whole city is decked out in coloured ribbons with pots of lucky basil placed on window sills.

GAY PRIDE

June/July Ⓦ www.ilga-portugal.pt
Lisbon's increasingly popular gay pride event (Arraial Pride) changes venues but has recently been held at Praça do Comércio.

SUPERBOCK SUPERROCK

July Ⓦ www.superbocksuperrock.pt
One of the country's largest rock festivals, with local and international bands at Parque das Nações and other venues.

NOS ALIVE

July Ⓦ www.nosalive.com
Another big-time rock festival at the Passeio Marítimo de Algés, on the riverfront west of Belém, attracting big-name acts.

JAZZ EM AUGUSTO

August Ⓦ www.musica.gulbenkian.pt/jazz
Big annual (Jazz in August) festival at the Gulbenkian's open-air amphitheatre.

CHRISTMAS (NATAL)

The main Christmas celebration is midnight Mass on December 24, which is followed by a meal of *bacalhau*.

NEW YEAR'S EVE (ANO NOVO)

The best place for New Year's Eve is Praça do Comércio, where fireworks light up the riverfront.

Public holidays

In addition to Christmas (Dec 24–25) and New Year's Day public holidays include Shrove Tuesday (Feb/March); Good Friday (March/April); April 25 (Liberty Day); May 1 (Labour Day); Corpus Christi (late May/early June); June 10 (Portugal/Camões Day); June 12 (Santo António); Feast of the Assumption (Aug 15); Republic Day (Oct 5); All Saint's Day (Nov 1); Independence Day (Dec 1); Immaculate Conception (Dec 8).

Chronology

60 BC > Julius Caesar establishes Olisipo as the capital of the Roman Empire's western colony.

711 > Moors from North Africa conquer Iberia, building a fortress by the *alhama* (hot springs), now known as Alfama.

1147 > Afonso Henriques, the first king of the newly established Portuguese state, retakes Lisbon from the Moors and builds a cathedral on the site of the former mosque.

1495–1521 > The reign of Dom Manuel I coincides with the golden age of Portuguese exploration. So-called "Manueline" architecture celebrates the opening of sea routes. The 1494 Treaty of Tordesillas gives Spain and Portugal trading rights to much of the globe.

1498 > Vasco da Gama returns to Belém with spices from India, which helps fund the building of the monastery of Jerónimos.

1581 > Victorious after the battle of Alcántara, Philip II of Spain becomes Filipe I of Portugal, and Portugal loses its independence.

1640 > Portuguese conspirators storm the palace in Lisbon and install the Duke of Bragança as João IV, ending Spanish rule.

1706–50 > Under João V, gold and diamonds from Brazil kick-start a second golden age; lavish building programmes include the Aqueduto das Águas Livres.

1755 > The Great Earthquake flattens much of Lisbon. The Baixa is rebuilt in "Pombaline" style, named after the Marquês de Pombal.

1800s > Maria II (1843–53) rules with German consort, Fernando II, and establishes the palaces at Ajuda and Pena in Sintra. Fado becomes popular in the Alfama. Avenida da Liberdade is laid out.

1900–10 > Carlos I is assassinated in Lisbon in 1908, while two years later, the exile of Manuel II marks the end of the monarchy and birth of the Republic.

1932–68 > Salazar's dictatorship sees development stagnate. Despite massive rural poverty, elaborate "New State" architecture includes the Ponte 25 de Abril, originally named Ponte de Salazar.

1974 > April 25 marks a largely peaceful Revolution. Former Portuguese colonies are granted independence, leading to large-scale immigration.

1986 > Entry to the European Community enables a rapid redevelopment of Lisbon.

1990s > Lisbon's role as Capital of Culture (1994) and host of Expo '98 helps fund a metro extension, the Ponte Vasco da Gama and the Parque das Nações.

2000–05 > In 2004 Lisbon hosts the European Football Championships. Fado star Mariza brings the music to an international audience.

2005–2015 > EU leaders sign the Lisbon Treaty on Dec 13, 2007, agreeing a draft constitution. Ten new upmarket hotels open in 2014, adding to Lisbon's burgeoning hotel scene.

2016– > Socialist António Costa wins a controversial election with the support of the Communist party, vowing to "turn the page on austerity".

Portuguese

English is widely spoken in most of Lisbon's hotels and tourist restaurants, but you will find a few words of Portuguese extremely useful. Written Portuguese is similar to Spanish, though pronunciation is very different. Vowels are often nasal or ignored altogether. The consonants are, at least, consistent:

CONSONANTS

c is soft before e and i, hard otherwise unless it has a cedilla – *açucar* (sugar) is pronounced "assookar".

ch is somewhat softer than in English; *chá* (tea) sounds like Shah.

j is like the "s" in pleasure, as is g except when it comes before a "hard" vowel (a, o and u).

lh sounds like "lyuh".

q is always pronounced as a "k".

s before a consonant or at the end of a word becomes "sh", otherwise it's as in English – Cascais is pronounced "Kashkaish".

x is also pronounced "sh" – Baixa is pronounced "Baisha".

VOWELS

e/é: e at the end of a word is silent unless it has an accent, so that *carne* (meat) is pronounced "karn", while *café* is pronounced "caf-ay".

ã or õ: the tilde renders the pronunciation much like the French -an and -on endings, only more nasal.

ão: this sounds something like a strangled "Ow!" cut off in midstream (as in *pão*, bread – *são*, saint – *limão*, lemon).

ei: this sounds like "ay" (as in *feito* – finished)

ou: this sounds like "oh" (as in *roupa* – clothes)

Words and phrases
BASICS

sim	yes
não	no
olá	hello

bom dia	good morning
boa tarde/noite	good afternoon/night
adeus	goodbye
até logo	see you later
hoje	today
amanhã	tomorrow
por favor/se faz favor	please
tudo bem?	everything all right?
está bem	it's all right/OK
obrigado/a	thank you (male/ female speaker)
onde	where
que	what
quando	when
porquê	why
como	how
quanto	how much
não sei	I don't know
sabe...?	do you know...?
pode...?	could you...?
há...? (silent "h")	is there...? there is
tem...? pron. "taying")	do you have...?
queria...	I'd like...
desculpe	sorry
com licença	excuse me
fala Inglês?	do you speak English?
não compreendo	I don't understand
este/a	this
esse/a	that
agora	now
mais tarde	later
mais	more
menos	less
grande	big
pequeno	little
aberto	open
fechado	closed
senhoras	women
homens	men
lavabo/quarto de banho	toilet/bathroom

GETTING AROUND

esquerda	left
direita	right
sempre em frente	straight ahead
aqui	here

ali	there
perto	near
longe	far
Onde é...	Where is ...
a estação de camionetas?	the bus station?
a paragem de autocarro para...	the bus stop for...
Donde parte o autocarro para...?	Where does the bus to...leave from?
A que horas parte? (chega a...?)	What time does it leave? (arrive at...?)
Pare aqui por favor	Stop here please
bilhete (para)	ticket (to)
ida e volta	round trip

COMMON SIGNS

aberto	open
fechado	closed
entrada	entrance
saída	exit
puxe	pull
empurre	push
elevador	lift
pré-pagamento	pay in advance
perigo/perigoso	danger/ous
proibido estacionar	no parking
obras	(road) works

ACCOMMODATION

Queria um quarto	I'd like a room
É para uma noite (semana)	It's for one night (week)
É para uma pessoa (duas pessoas)	It's for one person/ two people
Quanto custa?	How much is it?
Posso ver?	May I see/ look?
Há um quarto mais barato?	Is there a cheaper room?
com duche	with a shower

SHOPPING

Quanto é?	How much is it?
banco; câmbio	bank; change
correios	post office
(dois) selos	(two) stamps

Como se diz isto em Português?	What's this called in Portuguese?
O que é isso?	What's that?
saldo	sale
esgotado	sold out

DAYS OF THE WEEK

Domingo	Sunday
Segunda-feira	Monday
Terça-feira	Tuesday
Quarta-feira	Wednesday
Quinta-feira	Thursday
Sexta-feira	Friday
Sábado	Saturday

MONTHS

Janeiro	January
Fevereiro	February
Março	March
Abril	April
Maio	May
Junho	June
Julho	July
Agosto	August
Setembro	September
Outubro	October
Novembro	November
Dezembro	December

USEFUL WORDS

azulejo	glazed, painted tile
cais	quay
capela	chapel
casa	house
centro comercial	shopping centre
estação	station
estrada/rua	street/road
feira	fair or market
igreja	church
jardim	garden
miradouro	viewpoint/belvedere
praça/largo	square

NUMBERS

um/uma	1
dois/duas	2
três	3
quatro	4

cinco	5
seis	6
sete	7
oito	8
nove	9
dez	10
onze	11
doze	12
treze	13
catorze	14
quinze	15
dezasseis	16
dezassete	17
dezoito	18
dezanove	19
vinte	20
vinte e um	21
trinta	30
quarenta	40
cinquenta	50
sessenta	60
setenta	70
oitenta	80
noventa	90
cem	100
cento e um	101
duzentos	200
quinhentos	500
mil	1000

Food and drink terms

BASICS

assado	roasted
colher	spoon
conta	bill
copo	glass
cozido	boiled
ementa	menu
estrelado/frito	fried
faca	knife
garfo	fork
garrafa	bottle
grelhado	grilled
mexido	scrambled

MENU TERMS

pequeno almoço	breakfast
almoço	lunch
jantar	dinner
ementa turística	set menu
prato do dia	dish of the day
especialidades	speciality
lista de vinhos	wine list
entradas	starters
petiscos	snacks
sobremesa	dessert

SOUPS, SALAD AND STAPLES

açúcar	sugar
arroz	rice
azeitonas	olives
batatas fritas	chips/french fries
caldo verde	cabbage soup
fruta	fruit
legumes	vegetables
manteiga	butter
massa	pasta
molho (de tomate/ piri-piri)	tomato/chilli sauce
omeleta	omelette
ovos	eggs
pão	bread
pimenta	pepper
piri-piri	chilli sauce
queijo	cheese
sal	salt
salada	salad
sopa de legumes	vegetable soup
sopa de marisco	shellfish soup
sopa de peixe	fish soup

FISH AND SHELLFISH

atum	tuna
camarões	shrimp
carapau	mackerel
cherne	stone bass
dourada	bream
espada	scabbard fish
espadarte	swordfish
gambas	prawns
lagosta	lobster
lulas (grelhadas)	squid (grilled)
mexilhões	mussels
pescada	hake
polvo	octopus
robalo	sea bass
salmão	salmon
salmonete	red mullet

santola	spider crab
sapateira	crab
sardinhas	sardines
tamboril	monkfish
truta	trout
viera	scallop

MEAT

alheira	chicken sausage
borrego	lamb
chanfana	lamb or goat casserole
chouriço	spicy sausage
coelho	rabbit
cordeiro	lamb
dobrada/tripa	tripe
espetada mista	mixed meat kebab
febras	pork steaks
fiambre	ham
fígado	liver
frango no churrasco	barbecued chicken
leitão	roast suckling pig
pato	duck
perdiz	partridge
perú	turkey
picanha	strips of beef in garlic sauce
presunto	smoked ham
rim	kidney
rodizio	barbecued meats
rojões	cubed pork cooked in blood with potatoes
vitela	veal

PORTUGUESE SPECIALITIES

açorda	bread-based stew (often seafood)
arroz de marisco	seafood rice
bacalhau à brás	salted cod with egg and potatoes
bacalhau a Gomes Sá	dried cod baked with potatoes,
bacalhau na brasa	dried cod roasted with potatoes egg and olives

bife à portuguesa	thin beef steak with a fried egg on top
caldeirada	fish stew
cataplana	fish, shellfish or meat stewed in a circular metal dish
cozido à portuguesa	boiled casserole of meat and beans, served with rice and vegetables
feijoada	bean stew with meat and vegetables
migas	meat or fish in a bready garlic sauce
porco à alentejana	pork cooked with clams

SNACKS AND DESSERTS

arroz doce	rice pudding
bifana	steak sandwich
bolo	cake
gelado	ice cream
pastéis de bacalhau	dried cod cakes
pastel de nata	custard tart
prego	steak sandwich
pudim	crème caramel

DRINKS

um copo/uma garrafa de/da...	a glass/bottle of...
vinho branco/tinto	white/red wine
cerveja	beer
água (sem/com gás)	mineral water (without/with gas)
fresca/natural	chilled/room temperature
sumo de laranja/ maçã	orange/apple juice
chá	tea
café	coffee
sem/com leite	without/with milk
sem/com açúcar	without/with sugar

155

PUBLISHING INFORMATION

This fourth edition published March 2017 by **Rough Guides Ltd**

80 Strand, London WC2R 0RL

11, Community Centre, Panchsheel Park, New Delhi 110017, India

Distributed by Penguin Random House

Penguin Books Ltd, 80 Strand, London WC2R 0RL

Penguin Group (USA) 345 Hudson Street, NY 10014, USA

Penguin Group (Australia) 250 Camberwell Road, Camberwell, Victoria 3124, Australia

Penguin Group (NZ) 67 Apollo Drive, Mairangi Bay, Auckland 1310, New Zealand

Penguin Group (South Africa) Block D, Rosebank Office Park, 181 Jan Smuts Avenue, Parktown North, Gauteng, South Africa 2193

Rough Guides is represented in Canada by

DK Canada 320 Front Street West, Suite 1400, Toronto, Ontario M5V 3B6

Typeset in Minion and Din to an original design by Henry Iles and Dan May.

Printed and bound in China

© Matthew Hancock, 2017

Maps © Rough Guides

No part of this book may be reproduced in any form without permission from the publisher except for the quotation of brief passages in reviews.

164pp includes index

A catalogue record for this book is available from the British Library

ISBN 978-0-24127-031-8

The publishers and authors have done their best to ensure the accuracy and currency of all the information in **Pocket Rough Guide Lisbon**, however, they can accept no responsibility for any loss, injury, or inconvenience sustained by any traveller as a result of information or advice contained in the guide.

1 3 5 7 9 8 6 4 2

MIX
Paper from responsible sources
FSC
www.fsc.org
FSC™ C018179

ROUGH GUIDES CREDITS

Editor: Payal Sharotri

Layout: Nikhil Agarwal

Cartography: Katie Bennett

Picture editor: Phoebe Lowndes

Proofreader: Diane Margolis

Managing editor: Monica Woods

Production: Jimmy Lao

Cover photo research: Sarah Stewart

Editorial assistant: Freya Godfrey

Senior DTP coordinator: Dan May

Publishing director: Georgina Dee

THE AUTHOR

Matthew Hancock fell in love with Portugal when he was a teacher in Lisbon. He later returned to the country to walk the 775-mile Portuguese-Spanish border. Now a journalist and editor living in Dorset, he is also the author of the Rough Guides to the Algarve and Madeira and co-author of the *Rough Guide to Portugal* and the Rough Guide to Dorset, Hampshire and the Isle of Wight. He also contributes to the Rough Guides to England, Britain and Spain.

Additional accounts by Alex Hancock-Tomlin.

ACKNOWLEDGEMENTS

Thanks to everyone who helped, especially Vitor Carriço at Visit Lisboa, Heritage Hotels, Luke and Paula Tilley Pimenta, Amanda Tomlin for her invaluable support, and to everyone at Rough Guides, especially Payal Sharotri.

HELP US UPDATE

We've gone to a lot of effort to ensure that the fourth edition of **Pocket Rough Guide Lisbon** is accurate and up-to-date. However, things change – places get "discovered", opening hours are notoriously fickle, restaurants and rooms raise prices or lower standards. If you feel we've got it wrong or left something out, we'd like to know, and if you can remember the address, the price, the hours, the phone number, so much the better.

Please send your comments with the subject line "**Pocket Rough Guide Lisbon Update**" to mail@roughguides.com. We'll credit all contributions and send a copy of the next edition (or any other Rough Guide if you prefer) for the very best emails.

Find travel information, read inspiring features and book your trip at roughguides.com.

READERS' LETTERS

Thanks to all the readers who have taken the time to write in with comments and suggestions (and apologies if we have inadvertently omitted or misspelt anyone's name):

Claire Betty, Andy Bowman, Tiago Bueso, Gillian Clarke, Bruno Ferreira, John Field, Katherine Hewitt, Christophe Hore, Jackie Kennard, Joana Paranhos, Soygud, Chef Tanka, Melvyn Tully, David Verney

PHOTO CREDITS

All photos ⓒ Rough Guides except the following:
(Key: t-top; c-centre; b-bottom; l-left; r-right)

1 Alamy Stock Photo: Sean Pavone
2 AWL Images: Marco Bottigelli
8 Corbis: Frederick Soltan (cr)
12-13 4Corners: SIME/Sandra Raccanello (c)
17 Alamy Stock Photo: StockPhotosArt - Monuments/Sofia Pereira
19 Courtesy of Cantinho do Avillez: Paulo Barata (cl)
21 Alamy Stock Photo: Luke Peters
23 Alamy Stock Photo: Andy Christiani (b); Arthur Greenberg (t)
25 Embaixada (cr)
26 Alamy Stock Photo: Andrew Duke
27 Alamy Stock Photo: Kevin Foy (c); Nuno Fonseca (tr); StockPhotosArt - Urban Landscape/Jose Elias (b). **Dreamstime.com:** Phil Darby (tl)
28 Dreamstime.com: Martin Schlecht
29 Alamy Stock Photo: Dudley Wood (t); Kevin Foy (bl); Pictures CoTravel Picturestour Library (br). **Dreamstime.com:** Gvictoria (c)

36 Dreamstime.com: Ruslan Gilmanshin
37 Alamy Stock Photo: Peter Schickert
38 Alamy Stock Photo: Miguel Moya
39 Alamy Stock Photo: Alex Segre (t). **Dreamstime.com:** Mihai bogdan Lazar
45 Alexander Silva
51 Alamy Stock Photo: John Kellerman
71 Corbis: Demotix/Thomas Meyer (br)
83 Le Chat
88 Village Underground
93 Berardo Collection: © DACS 2016
112 Alamy Stock Photo: Mark Adams
125 Alamy Stock Photo: Dov Makabaw
128-129 Alamy Stock Photo: Hemis (c)
142-143 Alamy Stock Photo: Photolocation 3

Front cover and spine: *Monument to the Discoveries* **4Corners:** Olimpin Fantuz
Back cover: *Bairro Alto district, Lisbon* **4Corners:** Richard Taylor

Index

Maps are marked in **bold**.

A

accommodation 132–141
accommodation booking ... 135
addresses 147
Aerobus 144
airport 144
Ajuda 90–97
Ajuda, Belém and..... 92–93
Alcântara and
   the docks 84–89
**Alcântara and
   the docks 84–85**
Alfama 15, 44–57
**Alfama, Sé, Castelo and
   .... 46–47**
Almada 61
Aqueduto das Águas Livres
   102
Arco da Rua Augusta 34
arrival 144
Avenida da Liberdade .. 98–109
**Avenida, Parque Eduardo
   VII and the Gulbenkian
   .... 100–101**
Azenhas do Mar 122
azulejos (tiles) 53

B

Bairro Alto 66–77
**Bairro Alto and
   São Bento 68–69**
Bairro Alto grid 70
Baixa 30–43
Baixa and Rossio 33
Baixa grid 35
Barbadinhos Steam Pumping
   Station 52
bars
   A Ginjinha 21, 43
   Á Margem 97
   A Tabacaria 64
   A Tasca Tequila Bar 75
   Azul Profundo 115
   Bar Ba 64
   Bar Fonte da Pipa (Sintra)
      125
   Bicaense 65
   Café Paris 125
   Café Tati 65
   Chafariz do Vinho Enoteca
      .... 21, 75
   Chapitô 19, 56
   Chequeuers (Cascais) 131
   Cinco Lounge 76

Clube da Esquina 76
Decadente Bar 76
Doca de Santo 89
Havana (Parque das Nações)
   115
Havana Soul (Doca de Santo
   Amaro) 89
Intermezzo 65
Janela da Atalaia 76
Jonas Bar (Estoril) 131
Le Chat 83
Ler Devagar 89
Mahjong 76
Maria Caxuxa 76
Mini Bar 63
Ministerium Club 43
Music Box 65
Op Art 89
Panorama Bar 109
Park 76
Pavilhão Chinês 21, 76
Pensão Amor 65
Pérola 83
Portas Largas 21, 76
Portas do Sol 57
Povo 65
República da Cerveja 115
River Lounge Bar 115
Sétimo Céu 77
Sol e Pesca 65
Solar do Vinho do Porto 77
bars (by area)
   Alcântara and the docks.... 89
   Alfama 56
   Avenida, Parque Eduardo VII
      and the Gulbenkian 109
   Bairro Alto 75
   Baixa and Rossio 43
   Belém and Ajuda 97
   Cais do Sodré 65
   Cascais and Estoril 131
   Chiado 65
   Lapa 83
   Lisbon coast 131
   Parque das Nações 115
   Santos 83
   The Sé, Castelo and Alfama
      56
   Sintra 125
   Sintra coast 125
Basílica da Estrela 78
beaches ....see Praia
beaches, Cascais 128
Beckford, William 121
Belém 90–97
Belém and Ajuda...... 92–93

Benfica FC 106, 148
Berardo Collection 17, 93
bike hire 147
botanical gardens 71
bullring 105
bus (long distance) 144
bus routes 145
bus station 144
bus tours 146
buses 145

C

Cabo da Roca 123
Cacilhas 61
cafés
   A Brasileira 23, 64
   A Linha d'Água 109
   Adega das Caves (Sintra)
      125
   Antiga Confeitaria
      de Belém 22, 97
   Benard 64
   Café na Fábrica 88
   Café Vertigo 64
   Cafetaria Village 88
   Casa Piriquita (Sintra) 125
   Confeitaria Nacional 23, 43
   Cruzes Credo 56
   Cyberica 143
   Deli Deluxe 56
   Fábrica das Verdadeiras
      Queijadas da Sapa
      (Sintra) 125
   Galeto 109
   Leitaria Académica 64
   Lost In 75
   Martinho da Arcada 43
   Museu Nacional de Arte
      Antiga Café 83
   Nicola 43
   Pastelaria Santa Marta 109
   Pois Café 23, 56
   Santini (Cascais) 131
   Saudade 125
   Suíça 8, 43
   Tease 75
   Versailles 23, 109
cafés (by area)
   Alcântara and the docks.... 88
   Alfama 56
   Avenida da Liberdade, Parque
      Eduardo VII and the
      Gulbenkian 109
   Bairro Alto 75
   Baixa and Rossio 43

Belém and Ajuda.............. 97
Cais do Sodré................ 64
Cascais.........................131
Chiado 64
Lapa 83
Rossio 43
Santos 83
The Sé, Castelo and
    Alfama 56
Sintra 125
Cais do Sodré 58–65
**Cais do Sodré, Chiado and
    .... 59**
Câmara Escura 49
Camões, Luís de 91
Campo Pequeno...............105
Campo de Santa Clara 50
Caparica.......................129
Capela de São João
    Baptista 67
car rental 146
Carnival 150
Cartão Lisboa
    (Lisbon Card)........... 145
Casa do Alentejo...............39
Casa dos Bicos 45
Casa das Histórias 17, 128
Casa Museu Amália
    Rodrigues....................71
Casa Museu Dr Anastácio
    Gonçalves 105
Cascais 128
Cascais 128
casino, Estoril 126
casino, Parque das
    Nações......................115
Castelo 44–57
**Castelo and Alfama, Sé,
    ....46–47**
Castelo dos Mouros,
    Sintra.......................119
Castelo de São Jorge 15, 48
cathedral (Sé) 44
Cemetery, English 78
cemetery, Prazeres 60
Cemiterio dos Ingleses 78
Centro de Arte Moderna José
    Azeredo Perdigão 104
Centro Cultural de Belém....92
Chiado 58–65
**Chiado and Cais
    do Sodré 59**
children's activities............11
Christmas (Natal) 150
chronology 151
churches............... see Igreja
cinemas 147
City Hall 35
climate 6
clubs (by area)
    Alcântara and the docks.... 89
    Alfama 56

Bairro Alto 75
Cais do Sodré................ 64
Cascais.........................131
Chiado 64
The Sé, Castelo and Alfama
    56
Coliseu dos Recreios 39
Convento dos Capuchos.... 123
Convento do Carmo............67
Cook, Sir Francis 121
Costa da Caparica............129
crime 147
Cristo Rei 61
Cruise Terminal 52
currency.......................148

directory 147
disabilities, travellers with
   149
Discoveries Monument 94
Doca de Alcântara............84
Doca de Santo Amaro.........86
docks,.................. see Doca
docks area 84–89
Dom Fernando II o Glória
    frigate.......................61
drinking ....7, see also bars
driving 144

earthquake......................35
eating ....7, 18, see also
    restaurants
electricity......................147
Elevador da Bica...............60
Elevador da Glória 38, 66
Elevador do Lavra 39
Elevador Panorâmico da
    Boca do Vento,
    Cacilhas 61
Elevador de Santa Justa
    ....37, 67
embassies and consulates
   147
emergencies...................147
Estádio Jose Alvalade 106
Estádio da Luz 106
Estoril.........................126
Estrela 78–83
**Estrela, Lapa and
    Santos 79**
Estufas (hothouses)..........104
events..........................150
events listings................147
Expo..........................110

fado............................52
families 11
Feira Internacional de
    Lisboa (FIL) 113
Feira da Ladra market........50
ferry to Cacilhas..............61
festivals and events 150
films 147
Fonte da Telha...............129
food and drink terms 154
food specialities.............155
football........................148
Casa Museu Medeiros
    e Almeida..................99
Casa Museu Siznes-Viera
    da Silva 102
Fundação Calouste
    Gulbenkian.................102
funicular railways
    .... see Elevador
funiculars (elevadores)
   145

galleries 16
gardens............... see Jardim
gay and lesbian travellers
   147
Gay Pride 150
golf.............................148
golf, Estoril 126
Gonçalves, Nuno..............00
Gulbenkian, Calouste........103
Gulbenkian, the.........98–109
**Gulbenkian, Avenida,
    Parque Eduardo VII and
    .... 100–101**

health 147
history 151
horse riding...................148
hostels 141
    Home Hostel 141
    Lisbon Lounge Hostel.......141
    Lisbon Poet's Hostel.......141
    Moon Hill Hostel...........141
    Oasis Hostel 141
    Pousada de Juventude de
        Catalazete (Oeiras) 141
    Pousada de Juventude de
        Lisboa 141
    Pousada de Juventude
        Lisboa Parque das
        Nações.....................141
    Travellers House 141

hotels 134–140
Albergaria Insulana 134
Albergaria Senhora
do Monte......................135
As Janelas Verdes 137
Casa Amora 138
Casa de São Mamede 136
Casa do Valle (Sintra) 139
Chalet Relogio (Sintra) 139
Chalet Saudade..................139
Double Tree Fontana Park
.....................................138
Eurostar das Letras 138
Farol Design Hotel
(Cascais)......................140
Heritage Avenida
Liberdade 138
Hotel Anjo Azul.................137
Hotel Arribas
(Praia Grande) 139
Hotel Avenida Palace........134
Hotel Avenida Park...........138
Hotel Baía (Cascais).........140
Hotel Bairro Alto 136
Hotel Belver Príncipe Real
.....................................137
Hotel Borges.....................136
Hotel Britania 138
Hotel do Chiado 136
Hotel Dom Carlos Parque...139
Hotel Lisboa Tejo..............134
Hotel Métropole 134
Hotel Sintra Jardim 140
Independente, The.............137
Inspira Santa Marta 139
Jerónimos 8......................138
Keep, The..........................135
Lisboa Plaza 139
LX Boutique 136
Memmo Alfama.................135
NH Liberdade 139
Olissippo Lapa Palace 137
Palacete Chafariz d'El Rei
.....................................135
Pensão Gerês....................134
Pensão Globo.....................137
Pensão Londres.................137
Pensão Nova Sintra...........140
Pensão Portuense 135
Pergola House
(Lisbon Coast) 140
Pestana Palace 138
Real Caparica Hotel..........140
Residencial Alegria 139
Residencial Florescente ...135
Sana Rex 139
São Saturnia
(Sintra coast) 140
Sheraton Lisboa 139
Solar do Castelo 136
Solar dos Mouros 136

Vila Bicuda (Cascais)........140
VIP Executive Éden...........135
York House........................137
hotels (by area)
Alcântara.........................138
Alfama.............................131
Avenida, Parque Eduardo VII
and the Gulbenkian......138
Bairro Alto and
São Bento....................136
Baixa and Rossio...............134
Belém..............................138
Caparica 140
Cascais............................140
Chiado and Cais do Sodré
.....................................136
Estrela, Lapa and Santos
.....................................137
Lisbon coast.....................140
The Sé, Castelo
and Alfama...................135
Sintra and around 139

Igreja da Assunção, Cascais
.....................................128
Igreja de Madre de Deus 53
Igreja dos Mártires 58
Igreja de Santo António........45
Igreja de Santo Estêvão 52
Igreja de São Domingos 38
Igreja de São Roque............67
information 149
internet............................147
itineraries 8

Jardim Botânico 71
Jardim Botânico da Ajuda ...96
Jardim da Estrela 78
Jardim do Torel..................39
Jardim do Ultramar............90
Jardim Zoológico (zoo)......106
Jardins da Água................112
Jardins Garcia da Orta 112
Jazz em Augusto..............150

language................. 152–155
Lapa 78–83
Lapa and Santos, Estrela
.....................................79
left luggage 148
Lisbon Card
(Cartão Lisboa)..............145
Lisbon coast............. 126–131

Lisbon coast........ 126–127
Lisbon Welcome Centre 149
Lisbon Story Centre 34
listings magazines............147
lost property 148
LX Factory 87

Macao................................87
Mãe d'Água 99
marathon, Lisbon..............148
Marina de Cascais 129
Mariza................................52
market, Cascais 128
markets .... see mercado
menu terms 154
MEO Arena 110
Mercado da Ribeira............60
Mercado Rosa Argulhas 89
metro...............................145
metro map
.... see pocket map
Miradouro da Graça 50
Miradouro de Santa
Catarina.......................70
Miradouro de Santa Luzia....48
Miradouro de São Pedro de
Alcântara 66
miradouros (viewpoints)......10
money...............................148
Monserrate 121
Mosteiro dos Jerónimos 15, 91
Mouraria..........................49
museums
MU.SA..........................118
Museu de Água
Príncipe Real...............70
Museu Antoniano 45
Museu de Arqueologia 92
Museu Arqueológico
do Carmo....................67
Museu de Arte Popular 91
Museu de Artes
Decorativas 48
Museu Biblioteca Conde
Castro Guimarães,
Cascais.....................129
Museu Calouste
Gulbenkian 16, 103
Museu do Carris................87
Museu do Centro Científico e
Cultural de Macau 87
Museu do Chiado 60
Museu da Ciência.............71
Museu dos Coches 95
Museu Design Moda 34
Museu da Electricidade 95
Museu do Fado..................52
Museu da História Natural
.....................................71

Museu do Mar, Cascais.....128
Museu da Marinha ... 17, 92
Museu da Marioneta...... 81
Museu Nacional de Arte
Antiga 17, 80
Museu Nacional do Azulejo
.... 53
Museu do Oriente............. 85
Museu de São Roque 67
Museu do Teatro Romano....48
Museus Nacional de História
e da Ciência................. 70
music festival, Sintra........ 150
music venues
A Baiuca 57
A Parreirinha de Alfama..... 57
Alface Hall 77
B.Leza 83
Casino (Parque
das Nações) 115
Clube de Fado 57
Hot Clube de Portugal   109
Luy 57
O Senhor Vinho 83
Tasca do Chico................ 77
music venues (by area)
Alfama............................ 57
Avenida da Liberdade 107
Bairro Alto 77
Lapa 83
Parque das Nações...........115
Santos............................ 83
The Sé, Castelo and Alfama
.... 57

N

Nautical Centre 110
New Year's Eve (Ano Novo) ...150
nightlife...7, 20, see also clubs
Nos Alive........................ 150
Nucleo Arqueológico...........36
Núcleo Museológico and
Archeological Remains ... 49

O

Oceanário (oceanarium) 15,
112
Olivais dock 110
opening hours 148
opera..............................148
Oriente station 144

P

Padrão dos Descobrimentos
.... 94
palaces .... see Palácio

Palácio da Ajuda................ 95
Palácio da Assembléia........71
Palácio da Citadela........... 129
Palácio Nacional, Sintra.... 118
Palácio da Pena, Sintra..... 120
Panteão Nacional 51
parking 144
parks ....see Parque, Jardim
Parliament building............71
Parque Eduardo VII 98–109
**Parque Eduardo VII and
the Gulbenkian,
Avenida........... 100–101**
Parque do Estoril.............. 126
Parque Florestal de
Monsanto...................... 96
Parque Mayer.................. 99
Parque Municipal da
Gandarinha, Cascais 129
Parque das Nações... 110–115
Parque das Nações 111
Parque do Tejo................113
Pátio Alfacinha 96
Pavilhão do Conhecimento
.... 112
Peixe em Lisboa 150
Peninha........................... 123
Pessoa, Fernando 36
pharmacies 147
phones........................... 148
police, tourist.................. 147
Ponte 25 de Abril............. 86
Portuguese specialities 155
Portuguese terms..... 152–155
post............................... 148
Praça do Comércio... 28, 32
Praça da Figueira............38
Praça do Império 90
Praça Marquês de Pombal
.... 99
Praça do Município...........35
Praça do Príncipe Real........70
Praça dos Restauradores ... 38
Praça de Touros (bullring)
.... 105
Praia da Adraga 122
Praia da Conceição,
Cascais...................... 128
Praia Grande 122
Praia do Guincho 128
Praia das Maçãs 122
Praia da Ribeira, Cascais
.... 128
Praia de Tamariz.............. 126
Prazeres.......................... 60
Presidência da República
(President's house).........90
public holidays................ 150
public toilets................... 149
public transport.............. 144

Q

Quinta da Regaleira,
Sintra........................... 119

R

railway, narrow, Caparica
.... 129
Rego, Paula...................... 128
restaurants
1º de Maio 72
A Campaneza 41
A Licorista O Bacalhoeiro... 41
A Mourisca 54
A Praça.......................... 88
A Tasca do Manel
(Sintra)...................... 120
Aqui Há Peixe................. 62
Arco do Castelo 54
B & B (Cascais)...............130
Borracão de Alfama 54
Barrio Latino 114
Beira Gare..................... 41
Bengal Tandoori.............108
Bico do Sapato........ 54
Bistrot 100 Maneiras......... 72
Bom Jardim, Rei
dos Franços................ 41
Bota Alta 73
Caldo Entornado.............124
Cantina LX 88
Cantinho do Avillez........... 63
Cantinho de São Pedro
(Sintra)......................124
Casa do Alentejo 41
Casa Liège 63
Casanova.....................5, 55
Celeiro 42
Centro de Arte Moderna....108
Cervejaria Farol.............. 63
Cervejaria da Trindade
................................18, 73
Comida de Santo........ 73
D'Bacalhau 114
Doca Peixe.................... 88
Eleven 108
Esplanada 73
Esplanada Santa Marta
(Cascais)....................130
Estado Líquido 82
Estrela da Sé 55
Floresta de Belém........... 97
Floresta Santana 42
Guarda-Mor 82
Guilty 108
House of Wonders............130
Hua Ta Li....................... 55
Incomum 124
Jardim dos Frangos
(Cascais)....................130

Jardim do Sentidos 108
João do Grão...................... 42
L'Entrecôte....................... 63
L'Entrecôte (Parque das
    Nações).......................114
La Paparrucha................... 73
Lisboeta.......................... 42
Louro e Sal 73
Malaca Too 88
Malmequer-Bemmequer.... 55
Marisqueira Santa Marta.... 108
Mercado de Campo de
    Ourique 82
Mercado Rosa Argulhas.... 89
Music Bar (Cascais) 130
Noobai............................ 75
O Barbas Catedral
    (Caparica)..................130
O Cantinho do Bem Estar... 74
O Cantinho de São José....109
O Pescador (Cascais).......131
O Solar do Bitoque 131
Páteo do Garrett (Sintra)...124
Pharmacia 5, 74
Picanha 82
Portugália....................... 97
Praia do Tamariz (Estoril) ..131
Prego da Peixaria 74
Príncipe Calhariz 74
Restaurant Regional de
    Sintra........................124
Ribadouro...............19, 109
Rio Grande....................... 63
Rota do Infante 97
Rui dos Pregos................. 89
Sabor a Brasil.................114
Santa Clara dos Cogumelos
   55
Santo António de Alfama ... 55
Senhor Peixe..................114
Solar de Embaixador 97
Solar dos Presuntos 42
Taberna da Praça 131
Tão................................. 42
Tasca do Manel 74
Tascardoso....................... 74
Tavares........................... 64
Terra.............................. 75
Tulhas (Sintra) 125
Túnel de Santos 82
Varina da Madragoa.......... 82
Via Graça 55
restaurants (by area)
    Alcântara and the docks.... 88
    Alfama.......................... 54
    Avenida da Liberdade,
        Parque Eduardo VII and
        the Gulbenkian 108
    Bairro Alto 72
    Baixa and Rossio............. 41
    Belém and Ajuda 97
    Cais do Sodré................. 62

Caparica 130
Cascais 130
Chiado 62
Estoril 130
Lapa 82
Parque das Nações..........114
Santos............................ 82
São Bento 72
The Sé, Castelo and Alfama...47
Sintra 124
river cruises 146
Rock in Rio......................150
Rodrigues, Amália 71
Roman theatre................. 48
Rossio........................30–43
Rossio, Baixa and 33
Rossio station 144
Rua Augusta.................... 34
Rua Cor-de-Rosa...............61
Rua Garrett 62
Rua das Portas de Santo
    Antão 39

S

Saint Anthony of Padua.......45
Santa Apolónia station......144
Santa Cruz 49
Santa Engrácia 51
Santo António festival
    (Santos Populares) 150
Santos.......................78–83
Santos, Estrela, Lapa and
    79
Santos Populares 150
São Bento 66–77
São Bento, Bairro Alto and
   68–69
São Vicente de Fora............50
Sé...........................44–57
Sé, Castelo and Alfama
   46–47
shopping...........................7
shops and markets
    A Arte da Terra 54
    A Outra Face da Lua 40
    A Vida Portuguesa 62
    Amoreiras shopping centre
       107
    Armazéns do Chiado.....25, 62
    Centro Colombo shopping
        centre........................107
    Centro Comercial Mouraria...40
    Centro Vasco da Gama
        shopping centre..........114
    Conserveira de Lisboa 54
    Cork and Co..................... 72
    Discoteca Amália 82
    El Corte Inglês 107
    Embaixada...................... 72
    Fábrica Sant'anna............ 62

Feira da Ladra 50
Galeria Reverso................. 82
Livraria Bertrand 62
Loja Portugueza 40
Luvaria Ulisses 62
Madeira House.................. 40
Manuel Tavares............25, 40
Mercado da Figueira......... 40
Mercado 31 de Janeiro 107
Mercado da Ribeira 24, 60
Mistura de Estilos 107
Napoleão........................ 40
Paris:Sete....................... 82
Santos Ofícios.................. 54
Sneaker's Delight............. 72
Solar Albuquerque........25, 72
Storytailors..................... 62
Xocoa 40
shops (by area)
    Alcântara and the docks.... 87
    Alfama.......................... 54
    Avenida, Parque Eduardo VII
        and the Gulbenkian......107
    Bairro Alto 72
    Baixa and Rossio............. 40
    Cais do Sodré................. 62
    Chiado 62
    Parque das Nações..........114
    Santos.......................... 82
    The Sé, Castelo and Alfama
        54
shops, opening hours........148
sightseeing tours 146
Sintra......................116–125
Sintra 117
Sintra, around 121
Sintra coast 122–123
Sintra Music Festival 150
smoking..........................148
Sporting Lisbon FC 106, 148
sports 148
stamps 148
stations, train..................144
Superbock Superrock 150
surfing 148

T

taxis 146
Teatro Nacional de
    Dona Maria II................37
Teleférico (cable car) 112
tennis 148
theatre................. see teatro
tickets, events 148
tickets, public transport ...145
tiles................................53
time...............................149
tipping 149
toilets.............................149
Torre de Belém 14, 94

Torre Vasco da Gama 113
tourist information 149
trains 144
tram routes 53, 60
tram tours 146
trams and funiculars
  (elevadores) 145
tramway (Sintra) 122
transport, city 144–146
travel agents 149
travel passes 146
tuk-tuk tours 142

V

Vasco da Gama 113
Vasco da Gama bridge 113
Vasco da Gama, tomb of 91
viewpoints 10

W

walks, guided 146
water 149

weather 6
wheelchair users 149

Y

youth hostels 141

Z

zoo 106

SO NOW WE'VE TOLD YOU
ABOUT THE THINGS NOT TO
MISS, THE BEST PLACES TO
STAY, THE TOP RESTAURANTS,
THE LIVELIEST BARS AND THE
MOST SPECTACULAR SIGHTS,
IT ONLY SEEMS FAIR TO
TELL YOU ABOUT THE BEST
TRAVEL INSURANCE AROUND

 WorldNomads.com
keep travelling safely

RECOMMENDED BY ROUGH GUIDES

www.roughguides.com
MAKE THE MOST OF YOUR TIME ON EARTH™

ROUGH GUIDES